Marie Antoinette

Reversal of Fortune

By Michael W. Simmons

Table of Contents

Chapter One: The Archduchess

"The model of kings"

On November 2, 1755, Empress Maria Teresa of Austria, aged thirty-eight, gave birth to her fifteenth child and eighth daughter. It was a busy day for the Empress, and bringing another child into the world was only one of the items on her agenda—during the lulls between contractions, she was signing documents and attending to affairs of state. The Empress had always been lucky in childbed: she delivered sixteen children in total, thirteen of which survived infancy, without suffering any undue injuries from the births. Infant and mother mortality rates in her own family were thus far lower than those of 18th century Europe in general. But even with so many successful births behind her, a mother's survival was never a sure bet, and perhaps that is why she continued to work from bed, undeterred by pain or discomfort.

Maria Teresa was a ruling empress, not a consort—
and she had come to her throne after a long and
bitterly-fought war to secure her succession. A
devoted mother to her growing brood of children, she
nonetheless claimed that her first children were her
subjects. It would not do to leave her affairs of state
in disarray merely because she had the misfortune to
succumb to the same fate as any common woman
laboring in a peasant's croft. She was rather like
Isabella of Castile, who also had to schedule the
births of her children around more important
matters—Isabella gave birth to her most famous
daughter, Katherine of Aragon, during the midst of a
battle against the Moors, descending from horseback
only long enough for the delivery to take place before
mounting the saddle once again. Empresses in the
old days held themselves to high standards; much
like women today, they were painfully conscious that
any failures in their leadership would be attributed to
the inherent weakness of their sex. This was
particularly true of Maria Teresa, whose succession
had been so bitterly contested. A sovereign queen or
empress could afford even less than her male

5

counterparts to be seen as weak; the fate of their nation rested on shoulders that were popularly considered to be too frail to bear anything heavier than the weight of an infant.

When the birth finally occurred around eight o'clock in the evening, the Empress was pleased to have brought "a small but completely healthy Archduchess" into the world, but she took only a few minutes' rest before returning to her other chores. (Maria Teresa's children were archdukes and archduchesses because, as sovereign of Austria, she herself was titled an Archduchess—her more elevated title of Empress derived from her position as head of the crumbling Holy Roman Empire.) It was the baby's father, Emperor Francis Stephen, who announced that his wife had been safely delivered of a daughter to the anxious courtiers who were gathered in the room next door to the birthing chamber. Once upon a time, the highest ranking courtiers would have had the right to be present in the room as the birth was taking place, but that custom had been done away with in Austria. In France, however, where Maria Teresa's newest offspring would one day give birth to her own children, the custom was still practiced. After the baby had been duly admired by her mother's subjects, she was promptly handed over to the care of a wet nurse. Noble ladies of the time scarcely ever nursed their own children, as this was thought to ruin the shape of a woman's breasts.

The baby was baptized the very next day, November 3, as Maria Antonia Josepha Joanna. For four generations, the Hapsburgs had named all of their daughters "Maria", to symbolize the family's special veneration of the Virgin Mary, but naturally, none of the archduchesses were called by the first of their Christians names, or the confusion would have been considerable. Maria Antonia had been named in the Germanic style, but French was the language of the civilized world, and in Vienna it was spoken as often as German—indeed, the thoroughly French Emperor Francis Stephen spoke no German at all. To suit the fashion of the time, the new Archduchess would be called by the French version of her second name: Antoine.

There is probably no woman in history more famous for the tragic manner of her death than Marie Antoinette. Indeed, most people know nothing about her, save that she was Queen of France, guillotined along with her husband and scores of other French nobles during the Revolution. Needless to say, this was not the fate that her mother, or anyone else, expected for her when she was born. Yet anyone inclined to search the life of Marie Antoinette for ill omens that might have foretold the disastrous and violent end of her life would be well supplied with the kind of material that superstitions are made of.

To begin with, the date of her birth, November 2, is celebrated as the Feast of All Souls in the calendar of the Roman Catholic church. It is the day of the dead, a solemn occasion, scarcely a suitable date for a royal person to hold grand celebrations. November 3, however, the date of Marie Antoinette's baptism, was safely free of any morbid associations, and this was the date she usually celebrated. Besides, most Roman Catholic and Eastern Orthodox persons of high birth tended to reserve their merrymaking for the feast day of their patron saint. For Marie Antoinette, this was

June 13, St. Antony's day, and no doubt the summer date was more congenial for parties than a birthdate, or baptismal day, occurring in the dreariness of late autumn.

There was another dramatic omen coincidental with Marie Antoinette's birth, however. Due to the slow rate at which news traveled, no one in Austria was aware of it at the time. On November 2, 1755, a great earthquake shattered the Portuguese capital of Lisbon, killing upwards of thirty thousand people. Not even the King and Queen of Portugal knew of the disaster until much later; they were in Vienna to attend Marie Antoinette's christening, as her godparents.

Looking over the circumstances of Marie Antoinette's birth, there is just as much reason to suppose that she should have lived a long and happy life as there are signs presaging disaster. Her parentage might well be called lucky—not only was she the daughter of an empress, but she was the product of that rarest of all things, a successful love match between two royal parents. Her father, Francis Stephen, the hereditary Duke of Lorraine, was closely related by blood to the royal family of France, though he was obliged to renounce his claims to all but the title of Lorraine in order to marry Maria Teresa, who had rejected an even more illustrious match to the heir to the throne of Spain in order to marry him. The Empress had a knack for getting what she wanted, and amongst the sovereign rulers of Europe in her time, she was considered a model of both kingly and womanly virtue. Her peers included the famous Frederick II of Prussia, who had very little use for women in general and despised Maria Teresa in particular, as he considered the rule of women to be an unnatural thing. No sooner had she taken the Austrian throne than Frederick, seizing the opportunity to win an easy war against a young, female sovereign new to her role, occupied Silesia, a narrow strip of land which in modern times borders Poland, the Czech Republic, and Germany. Possession of Silesia was contested by the European powers until after the end of the second World War, and in the eighteenth century, Frederick II seized it for Prussia. Hostile feelings between Frederick and Maria Teresa would persist through their reigns, and it would not be long after Marie Antoinette's birth before lines of alliance between the European powers would shift, placing Prussia on the opposite side of a powerful multinational Austrian-backed coalition.

Whatever the Prussian monarch thought of Maria Teresa, she was generally regarded throughout the rest of Europe as "the glory of her sex and the model of kings." Another of her contemporaries was Empress Elizaveta of Russia, daughter of Peter the Great, who is best remembered by history for having married her nephew and heir to Princess Sophie Fredericke August of Anhalt-Zerbst, later known as Catherine the Great. Elizaveta's ministers, comparing notes with their Austrian counterparts regarding the ruling styles of their respective sovereigns, were wont to remark in private that if only the Russian empress gave half the attention to affairs of state that the Austrian empress did, their jobs would be remarkably easier. Maria Teresa was immensely capable and immensely respected, and no one who knew her would ever have dreamed that, in generations to come, the glories of her reign would be forgotten by all save historians, while her youngest daughter would be a household name and a pop icon for centuries after her death.

The wheels which set little Marie Antoinette's destiny into motion began to turn when she was only six months old. Maria Teresa's great enmity towards Prussia, which was growing in military might under Frederick's rule, led her to seek an alliance with Austria's great hereditary enemy, France. Not only might Austria find powerful friends in Versailles, but the French had long been staunch allies of Prussia—that is, until Frederick sought an alliance with the English, hereditary enemies of the French. The result was the so-called Diplomatic Revolution of 1756, in which a complicated network of alliances sprang up to contain the Prussian threat. The alliance between France and Austria would at length be strengthened by Sweden, Spain, and eventually Russia. (Empress Elizaveta disliked Frederick II nearly as much as Maria Teresa did, partly because he had the same chauvinistic contempt for her as for the Austrian empress, and partly because he had attempted to plant a spy in her court in the form of Princess

Sophie's mother.) Against this five-fold alliance stood Prussia, England, and Portugal.

The French-Austrian alliance was strong, but not necessarily stable. The bonds between nations would need to be strengthened if the alliance was to endure over decades. Between monarchies in the 18th century, there was only one reliable method by which to cement such alliances, and that was by marriage. The logic behind such unions was simple: every powerful family looked out for its own best interests, no matter what sorts of treaties they had signed, but by producing a child who belonged to both families, it was easier to trust one another's intentions. Sometimes it happened that there was a need for an alliance, but no children to marry off, but that was not the case in 1756. At the time, France and Austria and Spain all had princes and infantas and archdukes to spare. All that had to be decided was which royal sons of which royal houses would marry which princesses.

Maria Teresa needed her sons for heirs, but she had many daughters. All the young archduchesses were eligible pawns in the game of royal marital alliance, save only for the eldest, Marianne, who, though she was considered highly intelligent and unusually well-educated, was her mother's least favorite child and generally regarded as being too sickly to marry. The other daughters were sure to make advantageous alliances, but marriage to a French prince was not necessarily the most obvious match an Austrian archduchess might make. Though French was the international language of diplomacy, and though French fashions and tastes set the standard for wealthy living, Austrians subscribed to the same stereotypes about the French that would be recognizable to readers of British tabloids today. The French were held to be rude, promiscuous, lazy, and addicted to luxury, more concerned with royal spectacle than good government. By contrast, the Austrians considered themselves to be efficient, hard-working, and modest, or at least not overly concerned with pomp and ceremony. On the French side, the Austrians were considered coldhearted, stiff, and lacking in taste or elegance. A Frenchman who married into the royal court of Vienna could be forgiven sexual dalliances—the Emperor himself had set the precedent there—but an Austrian archduchess marrying a son or grandson of Louis XV would have a harder job overcoming perceptions that she was not elegant enough to fit into the court of Versailles, or that she was insufficiently enticing to her husband to produce children with him.

Decisions about her daughter's marriages ultimately rested in Maria Teresa's hands, but no monarch arrived at important decisions free of outside influence. More often than not, they were influenced by their courtiers and ministers, who had their own agendas—or at least, their own ideas about how best to serve their country. Her own reluctant prejudice towards the French was softened by the earnest advice of her counsellor, Prince Kaunitz, who persuaded the Empress that by securing her French alliance through the marriage of one of her daughters to the French king's grandson, she would have a powerful friend at her back should she ever attempt to wrest control of Silesia back from Frederick of Prussia. And on the French side, an Austrian marriage was the dearest wish of Louis VX's foreign minister, the Duc de Choiseul. Yet even with powerful and influential ministers working to arrange a match between a daughter of Austria and a son of France, there was no particular reason to look upon the Archduchess Antoine as a likely vehicle for the ambitions of two nations. As the youngest of all her siblings, Antoine was the least important, and the least likely to have an interesting future—until circumstances turned her fate in a different direction.

The education of an archduchess

"Rather sweet, but uninteresting," is how how one biographer characterizes the opinion of the formidable Maria Teresa of Austria regarding her affectionate youngest daughter. Antoine was to grow up rather neglected, lost in a brood of more significant siblings; if she was frivolous, as she has so often been depicted, it was because she had been taught to dance, and play the harpsichord, but had never been asked to trouble her mind with serious matters. And there seemed little reason not to let the

Empress's youngest daughter amuse herself however she liked. In every European court, the children of the sovereign were ranked in importance, first according to their sex, then according to the order of their birth. Sons, naturally, came first; the eldest son would be his parents' principal heir, and if anything should happen to him, his younger brothers would follow him. But an eldest daughter was likewise the most important of her sisters, the one whom it was presumed would make the most illustrious marriage. Austria did not bar women from the throne absolutely, as France did; the eldest daughter, therefore, came after the youngest son in the line of succession. And life was even more uncertain in the 18th century than it is now. Men, even princes, might die of disease, or on the battlefield. There was always the chance that an eldest sister might be so unfortunate as to lose all of her brothers before they could marry and produce heirs of their own. Bag the eldest girl, the reasoning went, and there was always the possibility that one might bag a throne in the process.

The younger sisters were likewise valued in order of their proximity to their succession, and thus, an archduchess with many older sisters would never be considered particularly important by her family or anyone else's, no matter what her personal qualities might be. Yet even if Marie Antoinette was neglected in regards to her education, overlooked as uninteresting by a mother who had the futures of fifteen children to manage, she always looked back upon her years in the court of Vienna as happy, even idyllic. Maria Teresa's impressive reputation was founded on both substance and on appearance: the substance lay in the fact that she was truly a brilliantly capable monarch, while the appearance lay in the image she presented to the world of unparalleled connubial and domestic felicity. Maria Teresa once remarked that she would have led her troops into battle herself, if she'd had any time to do so between her pregnancies.

Yet empresses were caught in the same sexist double bind familiar to women today. If they wielded their authority too expertly, they were castigated as unfeminine and unnatural; if they modeled feminine virtues such as docility and submissiveness, their subjects panicked, because a nation was only as strong as its monarch. Maria Teresa expertly navigated this dilemma, creating a model for female sovereignty that would later come to be exemplified by England's Queen Victoria. As a mother ruled her children, protecting them, guiding them, and loving them, the empress would rule her subjects. And to prove she was up for the job, she produced a brood of royal children to preside over, a model in miniature for the country in general. To suggest that Maria Teresa was anything other than the ideal wife and mother would be tantamount to suggesting that she was other than an ideal monarch. Such suggestions were therefore never made, even by those of her children who might have had reason to consider the circumstances of their upbringing other than ideal.

The successful love match between Maria Teresa and Francis Stephen was, despite appearances, not entirely untroubled. Bringing with him the sexually permissive habits of the French court, he kept a string of mistresses and lovers, while at the same time remaining devoted to his wife and family. There was no inherent contradiction in the two sets of behaviors, to a man of his upbringing. In Vienna, extramarital affairs were not conducted openly, and in the early years of her marriage the emperor's philandering ways placed something of a strain upon the Empress. But it was of the utmost importance that she present an image of unruffled domestic happiness to the outside world, so she gradually learned to turn a more-or-less blind eye to his affairs. If Antoine's recollections of childhood subscribed faithfully to the carefully maintained image of her parents' marriage, it might not have been a case of selective memory. After all, she was the fifteenth child; by the time she was born, Maria Teresa had made her peace with the status quo. Her older children, perhaps, might have remembered less tranquil days in their own childhoods.

There was also the religious element to consider. As a faithful Roman Catholic bride of her era, Maria Teresa owed a certain degree of deference to her husband. Yet there was a limit to how deferential she could be without compromising her own authority as sovereign. Maria Teresa managed to successfully blur the line between wife and empress without losing focus. Her excellence as a wife and mother reinforced her excellence as a monarch; they were complementary, not contradictory roles. In private, whenever possible, she made a show of offering her husband deference. Francis Stephen had been obliged, on the insistence of Maria Teresa's father, to cede control over the lands and incomes of the Duchy of Lorraine when he married. But Maria Teresa sought to make it up to him by permitting him to continue styling himself the Duc of Lorraine, to surround himself with Lorrainer courtiers, and to emphasize to their children that they were Archdukes and Archduchesses of Austria *and* Lorraine. This indulgence probably cost her little. Her patience was more sorely taxed when Francis Stephen began conducting his affairs openly; but to Maria Teresa, the wifely submission she owed him included tolerating his dalliances with other women.

There is much that is fascinating in studying the dynamic that springs up in the lives of the more famous daughters of ruling queens and empresses. It seems inevitable that some kind of cognitive disconnect must arise in the minds of impressionable young princesses whose mothers wielded supreme authority, yet taught their daughters that their own destinies lie in submission, obedience, and docility. Isabella of Castile again comes to mind. Her daughter Katherine, affianced to Prince Arthur, son of Henry VII, was sent to the English court as a young teenager, firmly resolved to be as obedient and pleasing as her new father-in-law and young husband might wish. After Prince Arthur died and Katherine was later married to Henry VIII, she had to reconcile her duty as both a daughter of Spain and the wife of the English king. She determined that the duty of a married woman must be to place the interests of her husband above even the interests of her father. Yet when Henry VIII initiated annulment proceedings against their marriage on false pretexts, the submission Henry had always been accustomed to receiving from Katherine vanished. She fought, she resisted, she pleaded, she appealed to higher authorities—in short, she gave no ground to her husband. Had Katherine of Aragon been the daughter of a lesser woman than Isabella of Castile, would she have clung so stubbornly to her rights? Would Henry have been forced to divorce the English church from

Rome in order to obtain the marriage he wanted? Even keen students of history can only make guesses based on the evidence.

Maria Teresa was more powerful even than Isabella of Castile, and she lived some two hundred years after Isabella, in a time when it was no longer considered strange for a highborn girl to be well educated. She was well read, and possessed all the intellectual rebellion that education can breed. Maria Teresa seems to have placed special emphasis on instilling her daughters with the model virtues of a Catholic wife, as though by producing a crop of well-behaved, gently mannered girls she was proving to the world that her own position as sovereign had not given her the idea that women in general had a right to aspire to the same autonomy that she herself possessed. The material point, on which every female monarch who reigned between the Early Modern period and the Enlightenment had to keep at the forefront of her subjects minds was that kings, queens, emperors, and empresses were placed on their thrones by God. Who could say why God was sometimes pleased to raise a woman to rule over the heads of men? The divine right of kings held that monarchs were subject to the judgment of no one, save God himself.

Empress Elizaveta of Russia, Maria Teresa of Austria, Elizabeth I of England, Isabella of Castile—all of them were given access to supreme power because their royal births created a loophole through which they were permitted to escape some of the strictures imposed on their sex. But when it came to the education of their daughters—those who had daughters, at least—they took pains to clarify the distinction between the destiny God had selected for them, and the destiny which both God and tradition reserved for most women of royal blood. Neither Isabella's daughters nor Maria Teresa's daughters were their heirs; they were not raised to rule, to consider themselves exceptions to the settled order of nature. Yet Katherine of Aragon remains a household name, while Isabella of Castile has become an increasingly remote historical figure; likewise, Marie Antoinette's name is known to schoolchildren, while the name of her venerable mother the empress, is known only to those who delve deeply into history.

One might account for the fact that the daughters have become so much more famous than the mothers because they lived through more extraordinary events, during more extraordinary times than ever their mothers knew. But circumstances are not made only of extraordinary events; they are also made extraordinary by the people who inhabit them.

No one who knew Antoine while she was growing up regarded her as an extraordinary sort of person, but those who knew her best occasionally caught glimpses of the sturdy character and keen perception that would only become evident to the world in general after her death, when the circumstances of her final year of life became public knowledge. One of Antoine's tutors remarked that she was "more intelligent than is generally supposed; unfortunately, she has not been trained to concentrate in any way, though I feel it is well within her power to do so." She hated reading, disliked writing and geography and most other academic subjects that were put to her; but then, most children find it difficult to apply themselves to their school work unless they are motivated by their tutors to do so. And there was no special need to motivate the youngest daughter of the Empress. It was enough that she was pretty, sweet, and pleasing; for a marriage such as she was likely to make, these qualities would be sufficient to recommend her to her future spouse.

The first shadow of unhappiness to be cast over Antoine's childhood was the death of her father, Emperor Francis Stephen, when she was nine years old. Maria Teresa was devastated. The loving, doting mother of her early childhood was swept away, and what was left in her place was no longer the woman, but the Empress of Austria, whose chief consolation was her devotion to her people. Marie Antoinette, likewise, was brought up to understand that *her* chief duty was service to her country. For an archduchess, this meant reconciling herself, from an early age, to the fact that she might at any time be called upon to leave the home of her birth and travel to a foreign court, there to live for the rest of her life. It often happened that royal brides were betrothed when they were still children, then sent to be fostered at the court of their future husband, the better for her future in-laws to ensure that was raised properly, understanding the duties and expectations that would await her when she became queen. Nine was not too young for a royal child such as Antoine to be sent to a new country to live among strangers. The threat of such early separation from their families was the counterpoint note that ran throughout a princess's privileged existence: at almost any moment, for the good of her country, she might be banished to live among strangers.

Chapter Two: The Dauphine

The child bride

As it happens, Antoine was spared the fate of those princesses who were banished from their homes in early childhood, years before their marriage, to be brought up by strangers. Nonetheless, she was, by any modern standard, undeniably a child when she left Austria for the final time and set out for France to meet her intended husband. Antoine was fourteen when her marriage was arranged to Louis-Auguste de Bourbon, grandson and heir of the Louis XV of France.

All of Antoine's elder sisters stood much higher in their mother's regard than she did, and it had seemed to everyone that the Archduchesses Elizabeth, Amalia, and Josepha would play a much more important role in the empress's diplomatic schemes than either of their youngest sisters, Antoine and Charlotte. But then, in 1767, disaster struck the Hapsburgs: a smallpox epidemic in the palace killed the wife of Maria Teresa's oldest son, Joseph. The empress likewise was stricken with the illness, and for a time her life was despaired of, though she survived. A marriage had recently been arranged between Archduchess Josepha and the King of Naples, but before Josepha set out on her journey to her future husband's court, she went into the crypts with her mother to pray at the tomb of Joseph's wife. The tomb had been improperly sealed, exposing both women to the virus. Josepha was infected by the smallpox and died a short time later, not before passing the disease to her older sister Elizabeth, the great beauty of the family. Elizabeth survived, but was greatly disfigured by facial scarring; no eligible royal suitor would take her after that. Antoine was spared. By a stroke of luck, she had survived a mild case of smallpox when she was only two, making her immune to the more virulent adult form of the disease.

Maria Teresa was left with three marital alliances to arrange, if Austria's position in Europe was to be secure—one with the King of Naples, one with the Duke of Parma, and one with Louis Auguste, who had recently become Dauphin of France after the death of his father. Yet, where once she had possessed a stable of five eligible daughters to bargain with, only three were left to her: Amalia, Charlotte, and Antoine. Both Charlotte and Antoine were close to Louis Auguste in age. Charlotte was personally known to members of the French court, and it seemed to them that she was the Austrian archduchess most likely to be a success at Versailles. But Ferdinand of Naples, who had lost Josepha, had the right to choose which of her sisters should replace her. He selected Charlotte for his bride. Since Amalia was deemed too old for Louis Auguste, she was sent, very much against her will, to marry Ferdinand of Parma. This left Maria Teresa with only one daughter to offer the King of France's grandson and heir: the insignificant Antoine. "It was...the rapid fall of a series of dominoes that made Antoine the focus of her mother's attention," writes biographer Antonia Fraser. "For the first time the Empress properly contemplated the material she had to hand in the shape of her fifteenth child. It had to be said that in many respect, she found it distinctly unpromising."

Antoine was considered to be pretty rather than beautiful, with certain defects which must be corrected before she could be presented to the Dauphin of France as a bride. She had thick, fair hair and wide blue eyes, but her teeth were slightly crooked. This was rectified by a few months' use of "the pelican", an early form of wire dental braces. She had an aquiline nose and a protruding lower lip, the product of many generations of Hapsburg inbreeding, and her forehead was high, with an irregular hairline. Being only twelve years old, she was also short, skinny, and did not fill out the bodices of her gowns, but it was hoped that she would grow out of those traits; after all, she was still pre-pubescent. Any number of faults and defects were apparent to the mother's critical eye, but others found Antoine more than pleasing enough to appeal to a prince. "One can find faces that are more regularly beautiful," Antoine's tutor wrote. "I do not think it would be possible to find one that is more delightful." Above all, Antoine had a remarkable capacity for making people like her.

Yet still, Maria Teresa fretted. It seemed to come as a surprise to her that Antoine's education had been so poor. She was next door to illiterate, it seemed, and had never applied herself at anything except for music and dancing, which she enjoyed for their own sake, and Italian, which had been taught to her by an especially capable instructor. She wrote slowly, shakily, and with abundant misspellings and ink blotches, and she avoided reading as much as possible—lack of practice, fear of disappointment and failure, and slight nearsightedness probably all contributed to her deficiencies in this regard. Women of Antoine's station in life were not expected to be especially learned, but Antoine's academic abilities fell far short even of that low bar. The chief trouble was that no one had ever taught her how to concentrate on an unpleasant task long enough to master it. There is also the possibility that she had a condition that would today be recognized as ADD, attention deficit disorder—this would certainly explain the assertion of her future lady in waiting, Madam Campan, that there was nothing lacking in the Queen's intelligence, but in her conversation she tended to jump from topic to topic, "like a grasshopper". Whatever the true cause of her lack of intellectual attainments, they were especially to be regretted now, since Louis-Auguste was known to be a bookish young man. But no one had expected Louis-Auguste to become heir to the French throne at such a young age anymore than anyone expected Antoine of Austria to marry him. They would both have to make the best of the situation into which circumstances, and their elders, had thrown them.

Louis-Auguste

The man who was to become Louis XVI, the last King of France, was not born for his position. He had a father and two older brothers who ought to have preceded him in the succession. While the second brother died when their mother was still pregnant with Louis-Auguste, he grew up very much under the shadow of his eldest brother, the Duc de Borgogne, who was the sort of paragon that inevitably makes younger siblings struggle with feelings of inferiority. The Duc died when Louis-Auguste was seven, and in recognition of his new status he was promptly moved into the rooms that his brother had died in. He was also given a new tutor, who attempted to instill in Louis-Auguste the qualities required in a king— firmness of character was emphasized above all. But firmness was one quality in which Louis-August was naturally lacking, notwithstanding his intelligence and studiousness.

Physically, he was not the sort of bridegroom who could attract the notice of any teenage girl, had he been anything other than heir to the French throne. Antoine was told very little about the character or personality of her future husband, but the little she was told proved disappointingly inaccurate. Versailles, they said, was like a fairy court, beautiful and glittering and exquisite in every way; the Dauphin was likewise a fairy tale prince, elegant in form, dress, and manner. In appearances at least, Versailles would live up to the praise. But Louis-Auguste was another matter. He was even more nearsighted than Antoine, unable to recognize the faces of courtiers unless they drew very near. He was also, at the age of fifteen, running to fat. When he came to be married, he had absolutely no experience with women whatsoever, even though a great deal of extramarital dalliance would have been forgiven in the heir to the throne of the old Sun King, Louis XIV, who had elevated his mistresses, including the famous Madame de Pompadour, nearly to the status of queens.

More worryingly for his future happiness in marriage, Louis-Auguste had been raised to despise the Austrian alliance. Anti-Austrian feeling was prevalent at Versailles generally. Louis XV wasn't insulted that his grandson was to be married to the King of Naples' and the Duke of Parma's leavings. All he, or anyone else at Versailles, cared about was the fact that the bride was Austrian. The Dauphin must marry an Austrian, the King had decided, and he didn't especially care which archduchess was made available for the role. At the same time, he wanted the negotiations to proceed slowly, to leave things unsettled for as long as possible, in order to spare himself the headache of dealing with the complaints of his courtiers.

The Marquis du Durfort was dispatched to Vienna as Louis's new ambassador to the Empress in 1767. Instructed to placate the Austrians with vague assurances and demurrals for as long as possible, Durfort quickly discovered that the clever, iron-willed Maria Teresa was not one to be put off. She maneuvered him skillfully into requesting a portrait of Antoine to send home to his royal master; when the King complained that this was moving too fast for his tastes, Durfort responded plaintively that he was not the one setting the pace. But the fact that France had all but reconciled to receiving Antoine was signaled in the autumn of 1768, when Versailles dispatched a special tutor to Vienna to make certain that the archduchess was sufficiently schooled in the French language. The tutor, the Abbé de Vermond, was the same man who wrote that there could be no more pleasing face than that of his young pupil. He would accompany Antoine when she went to France, and serve as her confidential advisor for years. Despite the fact that he found Antoine's French in a deplorable state—Vienna was said to be a city in which everyone spoke three languages, German, French, and Italian, and the French that was spoken in Antoine's family circle was a pidgin of all three tongues—she was fluent after a year under Vermond's instruction. When she arrived in France, all that could be said against her was that she spoke with a faint German accent.

Marriage

At long last, on June 6, 1769, the Marquis du Durfort, officially authorized by his king, applied to Maria Teresa for the hand of her youngest daughter, on behalf of the Dauphin of France. Louis-Auguste was then fifteen; Antoine was six months from her fourteenth birthday. The youngest and most overlooked daughter of Maria Teresa's great brood of royal offspring was now to be raised above all of her sisters; as Queen of France, she would take precedence over nearly all her surviving siblings. The irony was not lost on Maria Teresa, who was extremely anxious over Antoine's perceived deficiencies of intellect, and worried that she was not up to the challenge of making herself popular at Versailles. "If one is to consider only the greatness of your position," the Empress informed Antoine, "you are the happiest of your sisters and all princesses." But her compliments and praises were inevitably peppered with criticisms and corrections. To the French king himself, she was almost brutally frank: "Her age craves indulgence," she wrote, and she asked him to look upon himself as Antoine's father, to guide and correct her when necessary.

The preliminary preparations necessary for the wedding of an Austrian archduchess to a prince of France were sumptuous, elaborate, and borderline mystical in their symbolism. Prince Kaunitz, who had done so much to bring the French-Austrian marriage into being, was partly responsible for the preparations, as was Count Khevenhüller, the Court Chamberlain. An Ambassador Extraordinary was selected from among Prince Kaunitz's assistants; Antoine's procession from Vienna to the forest of Compiègne, including the crucial moment of the handover, was given specially into his charge. The glory of Antoine's progress would be calculated to reflect the glory, wealth, and power of the Austrian empire. The French must be reminded what a prize they were getting, after all; it had been a long time since the two royal houses had intermarried, and the daughter of the Austrian empress was something more, something rarer, than the average princess. She was "a daughter of the caesars!", in the words of Louis XV.

Antoine was married at six in the evening on April 19, 1770, in the Church of the Augustine Friars, the same Austrian church in which her mother had been married and Antoine herself had been baptized. It was a proxy marriage, with her brother Ferdinand standing in the place of Louis-Auguste. Her brother, Joseph, now co-emperor with his mother, gave the bride away. The purpose of a proxy marriage was to solidify the alliance as quickly as possible, and elevate Antoine to her new rank as Dauphine so that she might begin to enjoy the benefits before embarking on the long procession to the French-Austrian border. Once the proxy marriage had been completed, Antoine was officially a member of the French royal family, and for the first time she was permitted to write to her husband the Dauphin and her grandfather-in-law, Louis XV. Maria Teresa also wrote to the French king. "Her intentions are excellent," she said of her daughter, "but given her age, I pray you to exercise indulgence for any careless mistake…I recommend her once again as the most tender pledge which exists so happily between our States and our Houses."

Two days later, on April 21, Antoine left Vienna. "Farewell my dearest child," Maria Teresa said, embracing her. "A great distance will separate us. Do so much good to the French that they can say that I have sent them an angel." Both mother and daughter burst into sobs; it was very rare that princesses who married into foreign royal houses ever returned to the land of their birth, or saw many of their family members again. Antoine and Maria Teresa knew it was unlikely they would ever lay eyes on one another again, and in fact, they did not. Then the procession—fifty-seven carriages long—got underway. It would take two and a half weeks of travel before Antoine would reach the point of handover on May 13.

The handover ceremony—the moment at which Antoine's feet left Austrian soil and touched down on French earth for the first time—was called the *consegna* in Austria, and the *remise* in France. The symbolism of the handover was poignant. Antoine was forced to say goodbye to every attendant, every friend who had accompanied her to the border, including her little dog Mops. The new French attendants who were waiting for her then stripped her of every article of clothing she wore, and replaced the Austrian garments with clothing of French make and origin. As Madame Campan explained in her memoirs, it was critical that the bride "retain nothing belonging to a foreign court (an etiquette always observed on such an occasion)". In 18th century Europe, every woman was regarded as a possession, belonging either to the family of her birth or the family of her husband. As the Dauphine of France, Antoine was a highly precious possession—and it was therefore the more necessary that when she emerged from the place of handover to be received by the King and the Dauphin, she appear to them garbed as a Frenchwoman. Antoine was undressed and redressed in the "Austrian room", then led into the handover salon to be presented to her senior lady in waiting, the Comtesse de Noailles. Much to the shock of the Comtesse, who was accustomed to the rigid hierarchy of protocol observed at Versailles, Antoine flung herself into her arms for an embrace. The Comtesse quickly extricated herself and presented her husband the Comte, who by right of rank was entitled to a ceremonial embrace from the new Dauphine. The message, though Antoine did not receive it immediately, was that her attentions, even her affections, were now considered precious commodities, to which members of the court had certain rights, according to their rank. True emotion played no role in such matters. A Dauphine was royal property, and time with the Dauphine was a reward granted in exchange for faithful service.

Antoine emerged from the place of handover officially French. Two days later, she would be married to Louis-Auguste. They met face to face for the first time at the edge of the forest of Compiègne, Louis XV arriving in a carriage containing only himself, his four unmarried daughters, and his grandson. On a specially prepared carpet spread out upon the forest floor, Madame la Dauphine, as she was now known, knelt before Louis XV, the man she had addressed in her letter as *monsieur mon frère et très cher grand-père,* "my brother and dearest grandfather" (all royals addressed one another as brother and sister). The Sun King was charmed and moved by her manners, and lifted her to her feet, presenting her in turn to her husband. Whereas Louis was still said to be the handsomest man in his court at the age of sixty, Louis-Auguste was awkward, portly, and tongue-tied. He embraced Antoine stiffly; the historical record contains no trace of whatever emotion he may have been experiencing during this encounter. His journal entry for that day contains only the uninformative line, "Meeting with Madame la Dauphine."

The wedding was a grand affair. Attendees of all ranks were admitted by ticket only. There were some 6000 of them in total. Weighed down by an enormity of jewelry—since Louis XV no longer had a queen, Madame la Dauphine was entitled to wear the finest, gaudiest, most expensive jewels that the French royal family possessed—she was married to Louis Auguste at Versailles. Marie Antoinette, as she would be known for the rest of her life, impressed onlookers with her remarkable composure and dignity of bearing. Louis-Auguste, by contrast, appeared either bored or sulky throughout the long ceremony. But when he placed the ring on her finger, his hand trembled, which would seem to indicate that he was merely nervous. The marriage contract was then signed, first by the King, then by Louis-Auguste, then by Marie Antoinette—and here, the proof of her indifferent scholarship was set down before the eyes of her new family for the first time. *Marie Antoinette Josephe Jeanne*, the French version of her names in full, was set down on the page in a peculiar, slanting line. Even today the weakness of her hand is apparent; the signature is shaky, the ink blotched, and the first "e" in *Jeanne* appears to be missing. Ink blotches were to be a hallmark of Marie Antoinette's correspondence, particularly when she was exchanging letters with her mother—and there would be many such letters in the years to come.

Since the Dauphin and Dauphine were technically already married before the ceremony, the real work of the evening was the bedding ceremony. Maria

Teresa, with her customary pragmatism, had given Marie Antoinette (and indeed, all of her married daughters) frank instructions regarding what was meant to take place in the marriage bed. She was therefore as well prepared as a nervous fourteen-year old who had just married a boy known to her for only two days could be on her wedding night. The couple were led their enormous bed by the highest ranking members of court. Marie Antoinette was given her nightgown by her attendant, the Duchesse de Chartres, while the King himself gave Louis-Auguste his. The young couple climbed into bed, and sat up against the pillows with the covers pulled to the chests while the Archbishop of Reims pronounced a blessing on their union and the courtiers knelt in prayer at the wooden railing surrounding the bed. Then the courtiers bowed, curtseyed, and backed out of the bedroom, as the curtain was drawn to a close.

Louis-Auguste and Marie Antoinette, husband and wife, Dauphin and Dauphine of France, heirs to the French throne, were now alone together for the first time. The expectation of their families, the court, and the people of both France and Austria was that they would immediately set about the business of producing an heir. But no heir was to be produced that night—nor any other night, for seven years to come.

Marie Antoinette at Versailles

The comparison of Versailles to a fairy court was more accurate than Marie Antoinette could have guessed—but the comparison is more apt if one thinks less of Grimm's fairy tales and more of the fairies of Celtic folklore, beautiful but treacherous otherworldly beings with strange customs that carry dire penalties for any misstep.

There is simply no contemporary comparison for the rituals surrounding the life of a King, Queen, Dauphin, or Dauphine of France in the 18th century. The King and his heir (and their wives) were more than individuals; an entire court of hundreds of royal and aristocratic hangers-on derived income, significance, and status based on how close they were allowed to be to the royal family. The very morning after her wedding, Marie Antoinette discovered how this system worked for herself. She was awakened by a senior lady in waiting, and apart from standing up on her own two feet, she was not allowed to do anything else for herself. The morning ceremony was called the *lever*. It was the right and the privilege of the other women of the court to perform every function of the *lever*. Marie Antoinette's sleeping gown would be removed by one lady. Another lady would replace it with a day shift. Yet another lady would assist her with washing, another would bring her drink, another would slip her feet into sandals.

This was anything but a streamlined process; if, while one woman was in the midst of dropping the day shift over Marie Antoinette's head, another woman of higher rank entered the room, the shift would have to be given to her. In the mean time, the Dauphine, who was meant to be honored by these attentions, was standing there naked and shivering, waiting for the ladies of the court to work out amongst themselves who had the best right to clothe her. It was not as simple as requesting, or even insisting, that she be allowed to dress herself. Being of service to the Dauphine—being one of those envied few who possessed Right of Entry, that is, the right to stroll into the Dauphine's chambers at any time of day or night—was their entire function at court. Their actual duties might not take up much of their time (and in fact, the woman whose *charge* it was to perform a specific duty might assign a servant to do it instead, if she deemed the labor to be beneath her) but their position at court, the respect which they were due from other courtiers, depended entirely on the Dauphine acknowledging and permitting their right to do things like kneel on a cushioned stool next to her seat at the breakfast table, holding a napkin at the ready. (Marie Antoinette rarely allowed herself to be glimpsed eating in public, but the napkin was held at the ready nonetheless.) And these were merely the ceremonies of the *lever*; the *coucher* ceremony, when the Dauphine went to bed, was structured similarly.

The purpose of the Dauphine's existence (and the Dauphin's, and the King's) was to exist in a public place. She was never to be alone for a single moment of the day. Privacy standards were, of course, very different in the 18th century, particularly amongst royalty; Marie Antoinette would have grown up accustomed to having servants strip her to the skin and dress her like a doll, to being bathed by servants, to having other people in the room while she used her chamber pot behind the modest barrier of a screen. She would not have found the constant attendance of her ladies to be as invasive as would a person accustomed to 21st century modesty standards. But even for a young girl who had grown up accustomed to life in a royal court, the formal ceremonies that shaped life at Versailles were difficult for Marie Antoinette to become accustomed to. She quickly grew homesick, frustrated by the formalities hemming her in on every side.

The fact was, the ceremonial life of Versailles had altered from its original purpose. The rituals of royal existence had been set in place decades earlier during the reign of Louis XIV, the so-called Sun King, who made himself the living centerpiece of all these ceremonies in the same way that the sun stood at the center of the galaxy, with all the planets revolving around it. But the ceremonies took on a life of their own. In the Sun King's lifetime, they had showcased his magnificence; after the Sun King's death, they demonstrated the standing and importance of those who surrounded the monarch, from Princes and Princesses of the Blood (persons directly related to the King) to persons of much lower status who had been given their *charges* as a reward for service. Louis XIV had been the jewel, and his courtiers the glittering setting that displayed the jewel to best advantage. By Marie Antoinette's time, however, Madame la Dauphine was more like a solitary candle burning at the center of a room full of mirrors: the closer her ladies could get to her, the more brightly they themselves would shine.

Because the members of the royal family lived such transparent lives, it quickly became common knowledge at court that the Dauphin and Dauphine had not consummated their marriage on the wedding night. Indeed, it would have been impossible to conceal the evidence if they had; Marie Antoinette's senior ladies would have seen the results on the bedsheets when they came to wake her the next morning. The sex life of the Dauphine, like her dressing and disrobing and all of her other "privy functions", were not considered private matters. It was of the utmost importance to the future of France that the Dauphine become pregnant and produce an heir for her husband as soon as possible. Marie Antoinette and Louis-Auguste were permitted the shield of bed curtains to hide their intimate relations from prying eyes, but that was the utmost privacy they could expect. Every aspect of their reproductive functions was observed, reported upon, and discussed openly at court. Marie Antoinette's menstrual periods were noted and conveyed both to the King of France and to Maria Teresa in Austria. Marie Antoinette's mother was receiving regular intelligence of her daughter's affairs from the Austrian ambassador to the French court, Comte Florimond de Mercy-Argenteau, or "Count Mercy", as he was known to the Dauphine. Marie Antoinette did not realize that he was spying on her on her mother's behalf, but he had been specially chosen by Maria Teresa to keep an eye on her.

Maria Teresa was consumed by anxiety for her daughter's position at Versailles, and she was in a state of borderline panic as the months wore on with no sign that Marie Antoinette and Louis-Auguste had got around to the business of attempting to produce a pregnancy. Louis XV, who by this time was enchanted with his new granddaughter-in-law, was not nearly as concerned, and decided that Louis-Auguste was not to be badgered. But Maria Teresa could not be as calm. An unconsummated marriage was a marriage that could be annulled by the church. Never mind that it was Louis-Auguste who was responsible for the lack of sex in their sex lives; Marie Antoinette would be blamed. The wife was always held to blame, particularly if she were a royal bride from a foreign court. Marie Antoinette was extremely popular at Versailles when she first arrived; her beauty, her freshness, her lack of affectation, and her manifest talent for making herself liked all worked in her favor. But at the same time, she was more than a person, more even than a Dauphine. Behind her back she was called *l'autrichienne*, a word which, in French, means "the Austrian woman" but also sounds enough like the word for "ostrich"—a gangly, ugly bird from a faraway land—for the title to be used in mockery. To all those who resented Austria and the French-Austrian alliance, Marie Antoinette was the living emblem of their distaste. Her position at Versailles, Maria Teresa knew, would not be completely secure until she had produced an heir. Unable to scold or cajole Louis-Auguste, Maria Teresa focused her criticism on Marie Antoinette. All men had voracious sexual appetite, went her reasoning; therefore, if her husband were not eager to sleep with her, there must be something that Marie Antoinette was doing wrong. "I cannot repeat it enough," Maria Teresa wrote to her daughter. "Never be bad tempered about it. Use caresses, cajolings, but without too much energy. That would spoil everything."

Maria Teresa's worries were not entirely without foundation. Though Marie Antoinette understood that her duty was to be pleasing, she could not force herself to submit entirely to the rituals surrounding royal life at Versailles. The ladies in waiting who attended her during the handover ceremony, the wedding, and for some months afterward, had been selected by the King on the basis of rank and favor.

As Marie Antoinette began settling into her new life, however, she increasingly preferred to gather her own favorites around her and shut out the "Mesdames", the older women who had rights of seniority to be in her company. Likewise, she saw no reason why she should live her life so completely in the open. Flouting the customs which gave women of high rank the privilege of entering her personal apartments whenever they chose, Marie Antoinette began stealing away with her friends in secret, to play cards and gamble and gossip. It was not apparent to her then, any more than it would be later, that such behavior struck courtiers as sinister. The entire purpose of having a Dauphine, of heaping gowns and jewels and honors upon her, was so that they might partake in the spectacle. Why should she wish for privacy unless she had secrets to keep? Perhaps she spent so much time alone because she had a lover— and perhaps that was why the Dauphin had not slept with her.

Maria Teresa was a politician *par excellence*. She understood instinctively that Marie Antoinette was in danger of losing favor at court if she did not conform more closely to expectations. The danger would only increase the longer she went without becoming pregnant. The fact that Louis-Auguste was the King's grandson did not mean that the King might not put him aside in favor of another grandson, should that person marry and prove his ability to sire heirs before Louis-Auguste did. A great deal of the Empress's anxiety no doubt stemmed from the fact that, never having anticipated that her youngest daughter would make such an illustrious marriage, she had never bothered to teach her the lessons of diplomacy and politics that a future Queen needed if she was to survive. As Empress, Maria Teresa knew the history both Austria and France; she knew the political situation in Europe generally; she knew the unrest that was growing amongst the French people. Marie Antoinette, however, was still a child, lacking any knowledge whatsoever of the outside world. The only job she had been trained for was to live a privileged life and bear children for her husband. She was, in the strictest political terms, a womb, clothed in jewels and silks. The more Maria Teresa wrote to her, admonishing her about her behavior, the more Marie Antoinette came to dread her letters. "I love the Empress," she remarked, "but I'm frightened of her, even at a distance; when I'm writing to her, I never feel completely at ease."

Her mother's letters contained one piece of advice after another: "In the churches remember all eyes will be upon you ... so remain as long as possible on your knees, to give a good example... Do not permit yourself any contortion [in praying]; it might savour of hypocrisy — above all to be avoided in that country." Louis-Auguste was devotedly pious, whereas Marie Antoinette was merely conventionally observant, so her mother's advice might have been needful in this instance. But there were other bits of counsel which must have made Marie Antoinette feel positively claustrophobic. "Listen to no one if you wish to be happy", ran one tidbit. "Have no curiosity; it is on this point that I fear for you," she wrote. "Have no familiarity with inferiors," she said, though the Dauphine had already learned that the common women of Paris, the "fishwives", had, by ancient tradition, the right to enter the palace and mill about at their leisure, even to wander through the Dauphine's own rooms when she was not present. "Reply agreeably to all the world with grace and dignity," Maria Teresa admonished. "You can if you wish."

Anxious though her mother's letters made her, Marie Antoinette was a dutiful correspondent, though she hated writing and was still very bad at it. (Her letters, still accessible via the Habsburg Archives, reveal the same shaky handwriting and ink blotches visible on the marriage contract.) Not long after her wedding, she began writing the replies which were expected of her. Letters from Maria Teresa were put directly into Marie Antoinette's hands by Count Mercy, who likewise forwarded all of Marie Antoinette's replies. The letter below was written by the Dauphine shortly after she celebrated her first "fête day" at Versailles, the feast of St. Antony:

"Versailles, June 14

"My Dearest Mother,

"I absolutely blush for your kindness to me. The day before yesterday Mercy sent me your precious letter, and yesterday I received a second. That is indeed passing one's fête day happily. On Tuesday I had a fête which I shall never forget all my life. We made our entrance into Paris. As for honors, we received all that we could possibly imagine; but they, though very well in their way, were not what touched me most. What was really affecting was the tenderness and earnestness of the poor people, who, in spite of the taxes with which they are overwhelmed, were transported with joy at seeing us. When we went to walk in the Tuileries, there was so vast a crowd that we were three-quarters of an hour without being able to move either forward or backward. The dauphin and I gave repeated orders to the Guards not to beat any one, which had a very good effect. Such excellent order was kept the whole day that, in spite of the enormous crowd which followed us everywhere, not a person was hurt. When we returned from our walk we went up to an open terrace and stayed there half an hour. I cannot describe to you, my dear mamma, the transports of joy and affection which every one exhibited towards us. Before we withdrew we kissed our hands to the people, which gave them great pleasure. What a happy thing it is for persons in our rank to gain the love of a whole nation so cheaply. Yet there is nothing so precious; I felt it thoroughly, and shall never forget it.

"Another circumstance, which gave great pleasure on that glorious day, was the behavior of the dauphin. He made admirable replies to every address, and remarked everything that was done in his honor, and especially the earnestness and delight of the people, to whom he showed great kindness."

In this letter, one can see how Marie Antoinette made a special point of emphasizing how pleased she was with Louis-Auguste. Whether these sentiments arose from genuine feeling, or whether she merely wished to emphasize to her mother that the failures of their sex life were not the result of any repulsion which a pretty young girl might naturally feel for a portly, withdrawn, inept boy, must be left to conjecture.

Marie Antoinette's letters are also interesting in that they seem to answer the historical charge made against her, that she was too stupid and unintelligent to fulfill her duties as Queen. Her writing touches only on familiar, domestic subjects, rather than high ideals or deep political intrigue, but it is nonetheless evident that she was a clear thinker, capable of significant insights, who could construct a clear and informative narrative when she troubled to put pen to paper. An excellent example of this lies in the famous letter which Marie Antoinette wrote to her mother about a month later, in which she describes the routine of her life at the palace. Her clear, concise description of her schedule of activities and appearances is as orderly and replete as that which might have been produced by any contemporary court historian:

12 July, 1770

"...I rise about nine or half-past, dress, and say my morning prayers, then I breakfast and go to see my

aunts, where I usually find the King. That lasts till
about half-past ten, then at eleven I have my hair
dressed, at twelve is my reception, and all may enter
who are not common people. I put on my rouge and
wash my hands before them all, and then the men go
and the ladies remain, and I finish my dressing
before them. At midday is mass; if the King is at
Versailles I go with him and my husband and my
aunts; if he is not there I go alone with the Dauphin,
but always at the same hour. After mass we dine, just
the two of us, before all the company, but that is over
in an hour and a half, for we both eat very fast. After
that I go to the Dauphin and if he has business I come
back to my own rooms; I read, I write, or I work, for I
am making a vest for the King, which does not get on
a bit, but which I hope, will be finished by the grace
of God, after a few years. At three o'clock I go to call
upon my aunts, where the King generally comes
about that time; at four o'clock the Abbe [de
Vermond] comes to me, at five every day the music
master for the harpsichord, or singing till six. At half-
past six I go nearly always to my aunts, when I do not
go out for a walk. From seven we play until nine, but
when the weather is fine I go for a walk, and then
there is no play in my rooms, but in my aunts'. At

nine we sup, and when the King is not there my aunts come to sup with me, but when he is there, we go to sup with him and await the King, who usually comes about a quarter to eleven, and when waiting for him I lie down on a large couch and sleep till his arrival; but when he is not there we go to bed at eleven."

Even as Marie Antoinette began to carve her own niche in the court of Versailles, gathering her favorites to her side and availing herself of the luxuries that only a Dauphine of France could access, the fact that she was not pregnant nor likely to become so at any point in the near future weighed heavily on her heart and conscience. Whatever Maria Teresa believed, her daughter was well aware that her chief duty, indeed the very purpose for which she had been born, was to provide the King of France with an heir. Her mother was by no means the only person who attempted to give her advice on how best to interest Louis-Auguste in their marriage bed, but she was certainly the most consistent, and the most difficult to ignore. After Marie Antoinette had been at Versailles for well over a year, she received a letter from her mother for her birthday, in which she learned that her sister Charlotte, now known as Maria Carolina, Queen of Naples, was pregnant. Charlotte was two years older than her, and had been married a little longer, but the reply which Marie Antoinette made two weeks later demonstrates a keen awareness that her sister had succeeded in performing the duty which she herself had failed at:

"15 November 1771

"Madame my very dear mother,

"I am deeply touched by what you so kindly wrote me about my birthday. I especially want to follow the good advice you give me, my dear Mama. ... I do not think I did wrong when I gave in to my impulse and told the little secret to M. le Dauphin! I did not sound reproachful, but he was still a little embarrassed. I still hope for the best; he really loves me and does everything I want, and will conclude everything when he feels less awkward...

"When I wrote to you, dear Mama, that I needed no advice when it came to behaving properly, I meant that I had not consulted my aunts. [I.e., the unmarried daughters of Louis XV, the aunts of her husband Louis-Auguste.] However friendly my feelings for them, they can never compare to those I have for my loving and respectable mother; I do not think I am blind to their failings, but I think that they have been greatly exaggerated.

"Although the condition of the Queen [of Naples] often makes me think about mine, I still share my dear sister's joy. Ever since the summer, the trips and the hunt have stopped me from reading regularly; I have still read something almost every day."

The mystery of the marriage bed

Why, precisely, was the marriage of the Dauphin and the Dauphine still unconsummated more than a year after their wedding? Why did it remain unconsummated until 1777, after they had been married seven years? Conjecture was rife, with various parties blaming either Marie Antoinette or Louis-Auguste, according to their natural sympathies and prejudices. Whichever side one was inclined to take, the court of Versailles whispered of little else. There were those who generously believed that Marie Antoinette, young as she was, was simply too naïve to perform according to expectations. Those who held this notion were unfamiliar with the extreme pragmatism of Maria Teresa, who had prepared her daughter fully for the realities of sex. Others, less generously, believed that the Dauphine, who was prone to "disappearances" (i.e., those occasions when she closeted herself alone with her friends and denied the ladies of the court their traditional Rights of Entry) carried on with secret lovers during her absence from court. Some believed that her manners in bed must be somehow repellent to the Dauphin. Rumors of physical deformity could scarcely gain traction, since any number of servants and highborn ladies had glimpsed Marie Antoinette's naked form during the morning *lever* ceremony—indeed, the impossibility of concealing deformities was one of the *lever*'s intended functions. But it was rumored that the Dauphine might be suffering "from a condition known in the court as 'l'étroitesse du chemin', a narrow vagina", while the Dauphin possessed a "bracquemart assez considerable" (an unusually large penis), which made intercourse between them impossibly painful.

Those inclined to place the blame on Louis-Auguste were rather harder pressed to come up with an explanation for his failure to perform. After all, the thinking went, what normal teenage boy would not avail himself of every possible opportunity to sleep with such a lovely young wife? Yet there were signs from the beginning that Louis-Auguste was anything but overly enraptured with his new wife's charms. During the wedding feast, the King had advised Louis-Auguste "not to overburden his stomach" on this particular night, to which the Dauphin had replied that he saw no reason why he should not, as he always slept best after a hearty meal—a reply which would seem to indicate that he had something other than sex on his mind that evening. About two months after their marriage, Marie Antoinette begged her husband to confide in her, and Louis-August told her that he was holding himself to a particular code of conduct for a short time that required him to abstain from sex, but that he would soon commence normal marital relations between them. But more time passed, and no consummation was achieved.

Speculation abounded that the Dauphin was impotent, or that he suffered from some kind of physical deformity which made erections painful. This last theory was considered the most likely explanation by the King. As one historian writes, "The idea that the dauphin might suffer from phimosis [a medical condition resulting in an unusually tight foreskin] was not new. The previous year, Louis XV had asked his grandson Don Ferdinand—another member of the family late to discharge his conjugal duties—if he had not had to undergo a minor, quite common operation which his cousin (the dauphin) might also require." The King had one of his court surgeons examine Louis-Auguste, but the surgeon "put the king fully at rest"—there was nothing abnormal about his grandson's genitals.

The belief that Louis-Auguste suffered from phimosis persisted on Maria Teresa's side, however. She refused to believe that the failures of the marriage bed could be her daughter's fault, and therefore the blame could only lie in some physical defect on the Dauphin's side. And indeed, the phimosis theory was the explanation accepted by the majority of historians for the last two hundred years, though there is some division amongst scholars as to its reliability. Some believe that the letters written by Count Mercy to Maria Teresa "leave no doubt at all that Louis XVI did not suffer from malformation". Yet during Louis-Auguste and Marie Antoinette's lifetime, the belief persisted that their sexual dysfunction was due to the "impotence of Louis and his cowardice in refusing an operation to correct a small physical malformation [phimosis]", and that the Dauphin's dereliction of duty in this regard also explained "the queen's neurotic instability". But Marie Antoinette did not suffer from "neurotic instability"—this was a lie fostered by seditious pamphlets printed in the decades leading up to the Revolution. And contemporary accounts and historians both agree that the Dauphin fully understood the importance of his having a child as soon as possible—he probably could have overcome his cowardice in such a cause.

The doctors gave conflicting reports. Some said that he did suffer from phimosis, but that it was due only to his youth, and that he would grow out of the condition as he matured, without any need for surgery. The Empress could not reconcile the information she was receiving from the King, Count Mercy, and Marie Antoinette, all of whom had their own version of events. She might well have been aware that her daughter's marriage was not the first marriage between a foreign princess and a royal heir which had been made barren due to undiagnosed, untreated phimosis. By the time of Marie Antoinette's marriage, Catherine the Great had been empress of Russia for eight years. Prior to that, she had been the Grand Duchess Ekaterina, wife of Grand Duke Peter—and their marriage had remained unconsummated for nine years. The old Empress Elizaveta, desperate for an heir, had treated Catherine and Peter like prisoners, making them spend every second of the day together under the watchful eye of an appointed guardian, in the hopes that the enforced intimacy would drive them into each other's beds. But these measures did not produce the desired effect.

Like Marie Antoinette and Louis-Auguste, Catherine and Peter had been married as teenagers; like Louis-Auguste, Grand Duke Peter was a harassed soul who suffered from feelings of crushing inferiority, especially in the company of his intelligent, dignified young wife. There are conflicting anecdotal reports as to how, precisely, the marriage between Catherine and Peter was consummated. However, one anecdotal account claims that the Grand Duke eventually confided in his advisors about the pain he suffered during erections, and that his advisors immediately recognized the symptoms of phimosis and begged him to submit to the brief operation that would rectify the condition. Catherine's son Paul, later Tsar Paul I, was born less than a year later. This account cannot be verified, however—and there are some historians who believe that Paul I was, in fact, the product of Catherine's sanctioned affair with a Russian courtier named Saltykov.

But comparing the marriage of Peter and Ekaterina and the marriage of Marie Antoinette and Louis-Auguste suggests another explanation for their mutual early failures to conceive heirs. Both couples were teenagers when they married; Peter and Ekaterina were sixteen, and Marie Antoinette and Louis-Auguste were fourteen and fifteen respectively. Both the Grand Duke and the Dauphin were immature, shy, withdrawn, and physically unattractive. The Russian court and the court of Versailles were both sexually permissive, compared to other European royal courts. And both of these inept royal princes, carrying the weight of dynasties on their backs, were intimidated by their lovely wives—Peter, because Catherine was so much his intellectual superior, and Louis-Auguste, because he feared Marie Antoinette's power to influence him in the name of Austria. He had been cautioned by his tutor, who was a vehement opponent of the French-

Austrian alliance, that the Habsburg women were domineering by nature, and that, if Louis-Auguste were not wary, he might find himself becoming a puppet king who served the needs of Austria over the needs of France. Under conditions of such unease and mistrust, with the eyes of hundreds watching their every move, what sexually naïve teenager could be expected to overcome their misgivings about marital intimacy?

Royal marriages between teenagers were by no means uncommon. The King, at least, seemed to understand where the real problem lay. After Louis XV was assured as to the health of his grandson's "generative organ", he left Louis-Auguste to get on as best he could. Marie Antoinette, however, enjoyed no such reprieve. The admonishing letters from Maria Teresa did not let up, even as the Dauphine ceased to be a child and became a young woman. Nor was there any respite after Marie Antoinette became Queen; if anything, the badgering only got worse.

Chapter Three: Queen of France

"I am greatly distressed. My daughter's fate will either be wholly splendid or extremely unfortunate. She is so young... She has never had any power of application, or ever will have."

—Empress Maria Teresa, after the death of Louis XV

"We are too young to reign"

"When illness comes to princes, flattery follows them to the grave and no one dares admit to them being ill." This was the observation of the Baron de Besenval, commander of the Swiss Guards in Paris, as the health of Louis XV began to decline suddenly and rapidly in late April of 1774. On the 19th, the King had gone out hunting, only to find when he arrived at the hunting ground that he was too weak to leave the carriage. He took to his bed when he returned to the palace of Versailles.

It was not immediately apparent what malady the King was suffering from. Fevers might betoken any number of illnesses, or be deadly in themselves; there were no effective treatments for infections in the 18th century. In public, courtiers reassured themselves that all would be well, and the doctors maintained the position that, though the King was very ill, they were by no means as yet in despair for his life. But the truth soon became evident. Smallpox, a veritable plague in 18th century Europe, had been suspected from the first sign of fever, but since the King had survived a bout of the illness when he was younger, no one had dared diagnose him with it. It was left for the King himself to notice the pustules forming on his arm and announce to his doctors, "It is smallpox."

Louis XV had always enjoyed robust health, but smallpox was almost invariably deadly in a man of sixty-four, even if he had a strong constitution. There was no longer any point demurring about the possibility of recovery. The announcement had to be made, and the country and the Dauphin had to begin preparing themselves for the King's death. The story put about to the people claimed "that the King had been out riding; and had, with his customary compassion and interest in things morbid, approached a funeral procession, and learned upon inquiry that they buried a young girl, dead from smallpox; and that his Majesty was then struck with the disease."

Smallpox was exceedingly contagious. The story that Louis had caught it simply from brief exposure to the body of a dead victim was perfectly plausible—after all, Marie Antoinette's sister Josepha had contracted smallpox after praying at the grave of her sister-in-law. The group of attendants waiting on the King grew much smaller; it was not worth the risk that one of them might also become ill and spread it amongst the court, or worse, the servants' quarters. As the King neared the end of his life, his family was forbidden to enter the sickroom. Rather than leave him to die without the comforts of family, Marie Antoinette volunteered to sit by his beside until the end. She had survived smallpox as a child and proven immune to later outbreaks, even amongst her closest family members. As the Comte Mercy wrote to Maria Teresa,

"In these first moments of so grave and critical a time, it was necessary to decide whether the Dauphine should ask permission to stay with the King, or to remain with the Dauphin. Each alternative has its merits and demerits. I have suggested that the Dauphin should decide; and at the moment I write I do not know what is resolved... The Dauphine will no doubt tell your Majesty, but in the meantime it is certain that her Royal Highness has offered to shut herself up with the King; and she has at least the merit of having made the offer of sacrifice."

Her sacrificial gesture was denied, however. The King himself ordered the Dauphin and Dauphine both to stay away from his bedchamber, lest they too become ill. Marie Antoinette kept vigil with Louis-Auguste during Louis XV's final hours. "In so critical and delicate a conjunction" wrote Count Mercy to Maria Teresa, "the Dauphine has behaved like an angel; and

I cannot forbear expressing my admiration for her piety, prudence, and intelligence. The public is delighted with her conduct, and with just cause."

On the afternoon of May 10, 1774, a small crowd of courtiers stood outside the King's bedroom, their eyes trained on the flame of a tall candle that burned in his window. So long as the candle burned, the King lived; when he died, his doctor would snuff it out. The candle was extinguished at 3 p.m. Marie Antoinette and Louis-Auguste were praying together in the Dauphine's rooms at the time, and did not discover what had happened until they heard a strange roar, like a stampede, coming from the far side of the palace. At the moment the King was pronounced dead, the crowd of courtiers had fled the vicinity of his sickroom. Most were fleeing in the direction of the Dauphine's chambers; everyone wished to be the first to pay their compliments to the new King and Queen. Others simply fled the palace; it would not have been dutiful to forsake the King while he was dying, but now that he was dead, everyone was eager to flee the site of possible contagion as swiftly as possible.

Queen Marie Antoinette and her husband, King Louis XVI, looked at each other with tears brimming in their eyes, then fell to their knees and prayed together: "O God guide us, protect us. We are too young to reign." The Queen was nineteen years old; the King, only 20. After the senior courtiers had presented themselves to the new sovereign and his wife, there was a general exodus from Versailles, lest the smallpox contagion spread. There was considerable fear that Louis-Auguste might be infected, as he had never been inoculated nor had he had the disease as a child. The death of the old King was a misfortune; the death of Louis XVI, who still, after five years of marriage, had no heir, would have been a catastrophe. The entire royal family, and most of the court, made for the palace at Choisy, about five miles outside of Paris. Meanwhile, the remains of the late King were hastily sealed out of fear of further infection. They were conveyed at breakneck speed to the cathedral of St. Denis, there to be safely entombed.

A new beginning

Because Louis XV had been King for 59 of his 64 years—he ascended the throne at the age of 5, in 1715—there were few people still living at the time of his death who could remember the last time there had been a new King in France. As is usually the case when a country has endured a long period of hardship, the change of regime was very welcome, rather like a bonus New Years' celebration. Jewelers in Paris began to make a fortune off the sale of "mourning snuffboxes" adorned with a portrait of Marie Antoinette in her mourning finery. The inscription along the bottom of the portrait read "Consolation in mourning." Louis XVI (he dropped the "Auguste" from his name as soon as he became King) and Marie Antoinette were crowned amidst an enormous surge of popularity. They were young, the Queen was beautiful, both were healthy, and in an age where the longevity of the sovereign was popularly supposed to lead to an equally long period of domestic stability, the people of France greeted their new sovereign with enthusiasm. The undercurrent of all the rejoicing was the hope that the new King and Queen would at long last do something to alleviate the suffering of the people, who were laboring under crippling taxation and food shortages.

If the people of France were overjoyed by the coronation of the new King in June of 1775, the King himself did not share their enthusiasm. It was obvious, to his ministers and to himself, that he had not been adequately prepared by his grandfather for the burden of rule. He was intelligent, well-read, and did not lack understanding; he was equipped with all the necessary intellectual tools to assess situations and make wise decisions. But a ruling monarch must possess something more than this; he must be the master of all those who surrounded him. The traditional regnal qualities of haughtiness, authority, and majesty—qualities which separate the King from ordinary mortals and reinforce his special status as one of the few men on earth who are answerable to no one but God—were denied to Louis. There was "nothing haughty or regal in his bearing," remarked one courtier. "He gives the appearance of a peasant waddling behind his plow."

The unfortunate fact of the matter was that Louis had been too dominated, too neglected, and too unloved during his childhood to feel any confidence in his capacity to rule. And lack of self-confidence is almost invariably fatal in kings. They are at all times surrounded by people with agendas—people who are themselves dominant by nature, since otherwise they would never have managed to position themselves near enough to influence the King. When a king, like Louis, was ponderous, awkward, and irresolute, the best that could be hoped for was that he would swiftly fall under the influence of a highly capable minister who could rule the country through him. But would he fall under the influence of a truly capable minister with the best interests of the nation at heart, or would he merely capitulate to the person best capable of overriding him with force of personality? It was too early in his reign for anyone to be sure.

The Queen was as different from the new King in character as she was in physical appearance. Where he was awkward, she was graceful; where he was ponderous, she acted on emotions; where he was irresolute, she was always quick to make up her mind. These were the very qualities for which he had feared her, when they were first married; he had been warned that with a personality like his, he must be very careful whom he allowed himself to be influenced by, and there was no doubt that a woman such as Marie Antoinette could manipulate him if she wished. But by the time of his accession, Louis no longer feared that his wife was a secret agent for the Austrian empire who would attempt to sway him against acting in France's best interests. He trusted her enough by now that she might have influenced him politically, had she wished. But instead of attempting to exert any influence over Louis's government, she did exactly the opposite. She threw herself into the privileges of being Queen with what one historian describes as the gusto of "a teenager with a new credit card".

Louis and Marie Antoinette gradually, and almost accidentally, began to lead almost entirely separate lives. Their sex life was still nonexistent, so the King, who was an early riser, did not demand that the Queen share his bed; and since Marie Antoinette preferred to stay up late and sleep well into the afternoon, their schedules scarcely overlapped save for a few hours in the evening. Louis was busy trying to learn the business of being a king, while Marie Antoinette was spending her nights in Paris attending opera, the theater, and masked balls. Louis's preferred pastime was hunting just after dawn, and metalworking. Marie Antoinette made a game attempt to involve herself in his pastimes, in order to overcome his shyness and kindle his interest in their marriage bed, but she was not very successful. "I do not look well beside a forge," she said ruefully, after visiting Louis at his smithy. Louis did not demand that Marie Antoinette accommodate her amusements to suit him. He let her do exactly as she liked, and that included allowing her to spend as much money as she liked.

Still writing regular letters to her daughter, Maria Teresa had a new subject on which to rebuke her, though she never forgot the subject of the marriage bed for very long. Unlike Marie Antoinette, who neither knew of nor cared for anything that happened outside the charmed royal sphere in which she had existed her whole life, Maria Teresa knew that there had been bread riots in France. And she knew what sort of gossip was spreading about the new French Queen. Between the regular reports that Count Mercy was still sending to her and her own informational channels, Maria Teresa knew that her daughter was gaining a not entirely undeserved reputation for frivolity. She was setting a new style for the court of Versailles, which was only expected of a new young Queen, but she was doing so in such an extravagant fashion that it was exciting comment. How long, people whispered, would the disquieted people of France tolerate the Queen's excesses, when so many of them were starving and breaking their backs to pay their taxes?

The truth was, Marie Antoinette had nothing to do except amuse herself. She would dearly have loved to expend her energies on looking after a family, but since the King could not provide her with one, he provided her with everything else she could possibly need to be happy. So much leisure time would have seemed like paradise to the peasants of France, who worked from dawn to dusk their entire lives, but to those with no other alternatives, so much idle boredom can produce deep depressions. *Ennui* must be avoided at all costs. Marie Antoinette might play cards alone in her rooms with her friends, and attend Mass twice daily, and attend meals with her husband, but there were still hours of the day that cried to be filled, and the Queen could get no relief from books. Instead, she held balls and masques and revels and feasts and amused herself in Paris as often as she could.

As Queen, Marie Antoinette continued to ignore the traditional hierarchy amongst her ladies in waiting, choosing to surround herself with friends she had made for herself—still courtiers and noblewomen, but ones she actually liked, rather than those who had simply aged into the office of companion to the Queen. The jealousy this inspired soon combined with the rumors about the Queen's scandalous spending habits, the court's anxiety about the continued non-appearance of a pregnancy, and the Puritanical suspicion so often expressed towards any pretty young woman who appears to be enjoying herself too much, to form a toxic stew of rumors. For once, Maria Teresa was fully justified in her alarm regarding her daughter's public reputation. Though it would be two years before the infection spread from the palace to the world beyond, once it did so, it would prove to be a death by slow poison for Marie Antoinette.

As always, some courtiers were convinced that the reason the King and Queen had not consummated their marriage was because the Queen was spending all of her time with other lovers. She could easily pull off such a deception, of course, because she spent so much time screened from the eyes of the court, and lived her life so entirely separately from the King. Those who were bitter about being denied their ancient Rights of Access wondered aloud why the Queen should keep them away, unless she was keeping a secret? The noble ladies ought to have been in the Queen's confidence regarding her marital relations with the King. She should be coming to them for advice and explaining the precise nature of the problem to them. There was no regard for sexual privacy, when it came to the bedroom habits of the King and Queen of France. In the absence of an heir, or even a hint of pregnancy, the court felt that it had a perfect right to know what it was Louis and Marie Antoinette were doing wrong. But on this point, the King and Queen were united. Now that his grandfather was dead, the King would not be discussing his relationship with the Queen with anyone. And Marie Antoinette was from Austria, where it was held that the French were sexually licentious to a fault and had crude, unpolished manners besides. She believed, quite simply, that her sex life was her own affair. The courtiers of Versailles could not seem to explain her attitude to themselves without resorting to the most sinister motives.

Marie Therese

In 1777, two years into the reign of the new King, the Queen received a visitor—Joseph II of Austria, her oldest brother, who had reigned as co-emperor of Austria with their mother since after their father's death. Marie Antoinette was delighted by her brother's visit, as it was the first time she had seen a member of her immediate family since she was first married. But Joseph's visit was motivated by more than sentimentality. He arrived in Versailles at the behest of Maria Teresa, who had charged him to find out absolutely once and for all what was preventing the King and Queen of France from getting into bed and producing an heir.

It had been seven years since last Joseph laid eyes on his sister, then a bride of fourteen. Laying eyes upon her once again, he found her a changed woman. Joseph wrote to his brother Leopold from Versailles that the now 21-year old Marie Antoinette was "an amiable and refined woman" who was "not quite grown up yet...little inclined to take careful thought, but [gifted] with insight which has often surprised me. She has, however, a strong preference for pleasure." He was, of course, referring to his sister's reputation for frivolity—her elaborate wardrobe and three-foot tall hairstyles and constant attendance at parties and balls were still a source of profound consternation to their critical mother. If Marie Antoinette were not distracted by so many amusing pastimes, the assumption ran, she might have done more to overcome her husband's timidity in bed.

In fact, both the King and Queen had turned to the problem of their sexual dysfunction with new alarm and determination since the death of Louis XV. Once again, there was some confusion regarding the exact nature of that dysfunction. When the King agreed to see a doctor in December of 1774, the Spanish ambassador, Count Aranda, made the following report:

"Some say the frenum is so short that the prepuce does not retract upon entry, causing His Majesty much pain and forcing him to curtail the movements necessary to complete the act. Others think a tight prepuce prevents the head of the penis from being exposed, making it impossible for His Majesty to have full erections. If it's a matter of a short frenum, this condition is found in many individuals, causing problems when they first become sexually active; but since most people have a stronger sex drive than His Majesty (a reflection of his temperament or inexperience), they manage -- with practice, a groan of pain and some good will -- to tear the frenum completely, or sufficiently to keep using it, so that gradually intercourse becomes normal. But when the patient is timid, the surgeon makes a small incision, doing away with the obstacle. If the problem is a tight prepuce, one could resort to an operation which at the king's age is more painful and severe, requiring a kind of circumcision, because if the rough edges of the lips of the incision are not made smooth, intercourse could be impossible."

Marie Antoinette wrote to her mother shortly afterwards that she did not expect anything to come of the doctor's examination. "I strongly doubt," she said, "that the king has resolved to go through with the operation. Unfortunately, the doctors are confusing him. My doctor thinks the operation is not necessary, but could be very useful. The king's doctor, who is an old fogy, says there many drawbacks to having the operation and an equal number of drawbacks in not having it..." The disheartened Queen explained to her mother the painful nature of the gossip that surrounded them: "We are in the midst of an epidemic of satirical songs ... the need for the operation is the main thing used against the king. I haven't been spared either: I've been accused of having a taste for both women and men ..." Two years later, in January of 1776, the King consulted a famous surgeon in Paris, but without results: "He said pretty much the same thing as the others, that the operation was not necessary and that all would be well without it."

Such was the state of affairs when Joseph II arrived at Versailles. After speaking with his sister, Joseph decided that he ought to take Louis aside for a frank, private discussion regarding his marriage. Marie Antoinette's doctors still considered her to be a virgin, despite the fact that Louis had claimed a "demi-success" in 1772 which had made Marie Antoinette "my wife" in truth. What he meant by this can be guessed at based on the fact that the servants had occasionally found "stains" upon the royal bedsheets, as though ejaculation had taken place, but not in the required location. The King's conversations with his brother in law proved revealing. As though feeling that he could speak frankly to the Emperor of

Austria as an equal, when such frankness was impossible with anyone of lower rank, he answered all of Joseph's questions readily and asked him for his advice. Joseph relayed the information he had obtained from this conversation to Leopold again:

"In the end, it's not a weakness of the body or spirit; it's simply that he hasn't had his 'let there be light' moment yet, his technique is still in the process of formation... In his marriage bed, he has strong erections, he inserts his member, remains there for perhaps two minutes without moving, withdraws without ejaculating, and while still erect, bids good night. It's incomprehensible. He sometimes has nocturnal emissions but always while lying motionless. He's satisfied, saying he does it only out of a sense of duty but has no desire for it. Ah, if only I could have been present once, I would have set him straight! He should be whipped until he discharges in anger like a donkey. My sister does not have the temperament for this and together they make an utterly inept couple."

By the time Joseph left Versailles in late May of 1777, "the Great Work", as it was referred to, was well on its way to being accomplished. The marriage of the King and Queen of France was finally consummated on August 18, according to the report of Count Mercy: "The king went to see his wife just as she was finishing her bath; the spouses were together for about an hour and one-quarter; the king demanded a commitment from the queen that what had happened between them remain a secret. The only exception was to be the primary physician, Lassone, who, informed by the king of all the circumstances, did not hesitate to affirm that the marriage had been consummated." Both Louis and Marie Antoinette were delighted. To his aunts, the Mesdames, Louis confided, "I delight in the pleasure, and I regret that I wasn't aware of it for so long!" On August 30, the Queen wrote to her mother in an ecstasy of relief: "I'm experiencing the most fundamental pleasure ... it has been eight days since our marriage was consummated. The act was repeated and yesterday it was more complete than the first time ... I don't think I'm pregnant yet but I wouldn't be surprised if it happened at any moment." Why Marie Antoinette declared the consummation to have taken place on the 12th of August rather than the 18th, as Mercy reported, is not apparent, but perhaps there was a more or less successful attempt that preceded the event attested to by the physicians.

It is scarcely possible to overstate the relief that Marie Antoinette must have felt now that she could reasonably expect to become pregnant soon. Her sister-in-law, the Comtesse d'Artois, wife of the King's youngest brother, had given birth to a son two years previously, in August of 1775. The Queen, and all Princesses of the Blood, were required to give birth in public, their deliveries witnessed by as many people as chose to crowd into the room. The purpose of the tradition was to ensure that the royal infant could not be stolen, or a substitute put in its place. The Comte and Comtesse d'Artois were among the King and Queen's most dangerous enemies at court, since the Comte looked and acted the part of a king better than his brother did. Once he had an heir, it would seem as if the future of the family rested in his hands. The Queen, required to attend the Comtesse's lying in, felt the keenest humiliation possible when the birth of a son was announced. So frustrated were

Marie Antoinette's maternal longings that she had adopted a little peasant boy named Jacques who had accidentally been trampled under the feet of her horse. The Queen supported his grandmother and four orphaned brothers and sisters for the rest of their lives and kept Jacques as a member of her own household, supervising his education and arranging his prospects for adulthood. The Queen was very fond of Jacques, but a peasant boy was not an heir.

Every month, when the arrival of her menstrual cycle made it obvious that she had not yet become pregnant, Marie Antoinette was filled with despair. Yet finally, April of 1778 commenced with no sign of the Queen's usual "indisposition", as it was delicately referred to. On the 11th of that month, Marie Antoinette wrote to her mother in hopeful excitement, though she warned her that nothing could be certain for at least another month. By May, however, the pregnancy was confirmed. Maria Teresa promised that on the next St. Antony's day, the saint would be "tormented" with her prayers that the child be a boy. The Queen announced her pregnancy to the public through an act of generosity: she asked the

King for 12,000 francs which would be used to free certain persons from debtor's prison. The persons singled out for this mercy were those who had been imprisoned because they could not afford to pay their children's wet nurses; any money left over would go to the poorest prisoners, those who could otherwise never hope to obtain their freedom.

In raptures, Marie Antoinette set about making all the usual practical preparations for the baby's arrival. First, the nursery apartments were selected—situated on the ground floor of the palace, the windows would admit plenty of fresh air and healthy breezes. Then there was clothing to make, a wet nurse to select, and an *accoucheur* (male midwife) to select. Her extraordinary happiness enabled her to turn a deaf ear to the gossip that was circulating around the pregnancy. For some time now, vicious pamphlets, containing pornographic engravings, had been circulating around the court; they depicted the Queen as being engaged in lewd acts while making a fool of the impotent King. When the Queen became pregnant, however, the barrage of libel did not end. People were too entertained by the pamphlets to stop reading them. Rather than acknowledging that the King had done his marital duty at last, the pamphlets speculated as to the identity of the "true" father. The Comte d'Artois was a popular candidate. One can scarcely blame Marie Antoinette for choosing not to diminish her happiness by paying attention to such filth, but within a few years' time, the preponderance of libelous material printed against her would begin to rock the foundations of her husband's throne.

For details regarding the delivery of Marie Antoinette's first child, there is no more expressive source than the memoirs of Madam Campan. In early December, she writes, "the Queen's laying-in approached; Te Deums were sung and prayers offered up in all the cathedrals. On December 11, 1778, the royal family, the Princes of the royal blood, and the Great Officers of State spent the night in the rooms adjoining the Queen's Bedchamber." The birth would not actually take until eight days later, on December 19th. The Queen felt the first *doleurs*, or labor pains, shortly after midnight, though she waited until half past one to ring the bell for her attendants.

"The etiquette," writes Madame Campan, "allowing all persons indiscriminately to enter at the moment of the delivery of a queen was observed with such exaggeration that when the obstetrician said aloud: 'The Queen is going to give birth!' the persons who poured into the chamber were so numerous that the rush nearly killed the Queen. During the night the King had taken the precaution to have the enormous tapestry screens which surrounded Her Majesty's bed secured with cords; but for this they certainly would have been thrown down upon her. It was impossible to move about the chamber, which was filled with so motley a crowd that one might have fancied himself in some place of public amusement. Two chimney-sweeps climbed upon the furniture for a better sight of the Queen."

The baby was delivered at 11:30 in the morning, and the Queen promptly fainted. ("This cruel custom," Madame Campan writes, referring to the practice of allowing so many strangers to attend royal births, "was abolished afterwards. The Princes of the family, the Princes of the blood, the Chancellor, and the ministers are surely sufficient to attest the legitimacy of a prince.") Several strong men rushed to the windows and tore away the shutters, which had been nailed shut; the rush of fresh air in the overcrowded, over-heated room quickly revived her. She had not, as everyone had hoped and expected, given birth to a new Dauphin, but to a daughter. The child's name had been chosen in advance, since royal infants were baptized the day after their birth: she was called Marie Therese Charlotte, in honor of her godparents, Maria Teresa of Austria and Charles III of Spain. Since females could not succeed to the throne under French law, the new princess was not the Dauphine. Instead, she was called Madame Fille-du-Roi, though by the time she was five this title had been truncated to Madame Royale. (According to the custom of Versailles, to be known merely as "Madame" or "Monsieur" was a privilege reserved for those of the very highest royal birth. Marie Antoinette had been addressed as "Madame la Dauphine" and Louis XV's unmarried daughters, the King's aunts, were known collectively as "Mesdames Tantes", or the Madam Aunts.)

When Marie Therese was thirteen years old, she asked her father whether he happened to know the age of the boy who had just become King of Sweden. Louis XVI replied that he knew it precisely, because he had been given word of it at almost the same moment he was notified that the Queen was being brought to bed with Marie Therese. He had, apparently, warned the Queen that she certainly be giving birth to a daughter, since it would be straining credulity to suppose that two kings might both have sons born to them in the same month. The princess, somewhat bashfully, asked whether her father had been very sorry that she was not a boy. Louis assured her that he was not disappointed in the slightest, which caused Marie Therese to burst into tears, and an admiring court to dab at their own eyes. It is impossible, however, that Louis was not disappointed that his firstborn was not a boy; having failed in his duty to produce a child for so long, he must have been hoping that his wife's first pregnancy would result in the necessary male heir. By the time Marie Therese was thirteen, however, she had two brothers and a sister. The anxiety over heirs had long since been satisfied, so it was no doubt easy for Louis to set aside the memory of those troubled times and tell his daughter a loving falsehood.

As for Marie Antoinette, she did not learn whether she had given birth to a boy or a girl until some hour and a half after her labors were finished. She had had a mild convulsive fit and possibly a slight hemorrhage which had rendered her insensible at first. When she woke again, she was told that she had a daughter; immediately, she burst into tears. Observers assumed she was distressed by the child's sex, but it is equally likely that the tears came from relief—not until that moment had she known for certain that the baby was alive and healthy. And there was nothing of disappointment in her first words to the baby, when she was finally placed in the Queen's arms: "Poor little one," she said, "you were not wished for, but you are not on that account less dear to me. A son would have been rather the property of the State. You shall be mine; you shall have my undivided care, shall share all my happiness, and console me in all my troubles." Influenced by theories recently put forth by Rousseau that children were healthier when nursed by their own mothers, Marie Antoinette insisted on feeding her baby at her own breast, much to the shock of the court.

The same scurrilous gossip which had been provoked by the announcement of the pregnancy made an ugly appearance at Marie Therese's baptism. The Comte de Provence, one of the King's brothers, halted the Archbishop in his ceremony to point out that the "name and quality" of the child's parents had not been formally announced, as was usual in the baptismal rite. The Archbishop had seen no need for such an announcement, considering that the child was the daughter of the King and Queen of France—but the Comte de Provence was deliberately invoking the lie circulated by the pamphlets that someone other than Louis had fathered Marie Antoinette's child. Doubts on that score were being entertained outside the palace as well. Again, the Queen studiously ignored the calumnies being spread about her. She celebrated her daughter's birth by selecting 100 "poor and virtuous" girls who were engaged to be married to "honest" young men, and giving them weddings at the Cathedral of Notre Dame and 500 livres apiece for their dowries.

Maria Teresa lost no time following the birth of her namesake before demanding that Marie Antoinette and Louis provide the little girl with "a companion", i.e., a younger sibling, hopefully a brother. Although the King and Queen would produce three more children—Louis Joseph, the long awaited Dauphin, born October 22, 1781; Louis-Charles, the Prince Royal, born March 27, 1785; and Sophie Beatrix, known as Madame Sophie, born July 9, 1786—their grandmother would not live long enough to greet their arrivals. Maria Teresa, Holy Roman Empress and Archduchess of Austria, died two years after the birth of Marie Therese. She went into a rapid decline early in November, and seemed to have some sense that her death was approaching. Her final letter to Marie Antoinette was dated November 3, and it contained greetings on her daughter's 25th birthday. She had not seen Marie Antoinette in over ten years, but in her letter she observed that, "Yesterday I was all day more in France than in Austria." She was confined to bed for five days before the end came, and during that time, she refused to sleep. "At any moment I may be called before my Judge," she said.

"I don't want to be surprised. I want to see death come." She died on November 29, 1780, at the age of sixty-three—a respectable old age, by the standards of the 18th century.

Marie Antoinette was "Devastated by this most frightful misfortune," as she wrote in a letter to her brother Joseph, now sole Emperor. "I cannot stop crying as I start to write to you. Oh my brother, oh my friend! You alone are left to me in a country [Austria] which is, and always will be, so dear to me... Remember, we are your friends, your allies. I embrace you." Her entreaties were not merely those of a sister clinging to an older brother over the loss of a parent. In the winter of 1777, France had made a formal alliance of mutual defense with the American colonies, supporting them in their bid for independence from England. Prussia had come to England's aid against the Americans; Austria was considering doing the same. "Remember we are your friends, your allies," was as much the plea of the Queen of France to the Austrian emperor as it was the cry of a sister to her brother.

Marie Antoinette had been married to the French Dauphin in 1770 because Maria Teresa wanted an agent at Versailles who would promote Austrian interests. Louis, his tutor, and the anti-Austrian faction at court had not been wrong about that. But like most princesses before her who had married into foreign royal houses, Marie Antoinette was becoming more and more French in her sympathies. While her mother lived, she felt obligated to try to live up to the Empress's expectations and promote Austrian interests when possible. After Maria Teresa's death however, things changed. The Austrian ambassador, Count Mercy, had cooperated with the Empress to influence Marie Antoinette. But Joseph II did not have the same relationship with Mercy; when he wished to communicate with Marie Antoinette, he did so directly. Though Joseph was old enough to be her father, he did not view his sister in quite the same childish light as their mother had done, and Marie Antoinette occasionally succeeded in influencing him. Certainly, Austria did not abandon its alliance with France for the English. "Our links with France are natural, advantageous, and infinitely preferable to those with England," Joseph assured his sister and brother in law.

When Marie Antoinette realized that she was pregnant again in early 1781, she decided to retreat from the life of the court. At Petit Triannon, her personal refuge, the Queen attended to the care and education of her children, leaving politics to her husband at Versailles. In one of history's bitterest ironies, this "disappearance" from the public eye, motivated by nothing more sinister than the desire to look after her family, would throw fuel on the fire of the rumors that surrounded her—the pamphlets which insisted she was a sexual deviant, a cruel, callous, neglectful mother, a mocking, shrewish wife, a secret lesbian, and a serial adulterer.

Chapter Four: The Affair of the Diamond Necklace

"Kept at ease by the consciousness of innocence, and well knowing all about her must do justice to her private life, the Queen spoke of these false reports with contempt, contenting herself with the supposition, that some vain folly in the young men above mentioned, bad given rise to them. She therefore left off speaking to them, or even looking at them. Their vanity took the alarm at this, and the pleasure of revenge induced them either to say, or to leave others to think, that they were unfortunate enough to please no longer. Other young coxcombs, placing them selves near the private box, which the Queen occupied incognita, when she attended the public theatre at Versailles, had the presumption to imagine that they were noticed by her; and I have known such notions entertained, merely on account of the Queen's requesting one of those gentlemen to enquire behind the scenes, whether it would be long before the commencement of the second piece."

—from the Memoirs of Mme. Campan

Madame Deficit

By the early 1780s, Marie Antoinette, who had been
so popular during the first two years of her reign, was
rapidly losing the love of the French people. Contrary
to common assumption, the court of Versailles had
always been decadent—Marie Antoinette was
certainly no worse than the Sun King had been when
it came to profligate spending—and French support
for the American Revolution was far more to blame
for the massive national debt than the bills the Queen
was running up. But the people needed someone to
blame; in fact, they seemed to need someone to hate.
And as a woman and a foreigner, Marie Antoinette
made a convenient scapegoat.

The pornographic pamphlet industry which made
Marie Antoinette its particular target had pilloried
other women in the past; the previous object of their
lurid speculations and inventions had been the
Comtesse du Barry, the last beloved mistress of Louis
XV. But when du Barry was sent away from the
palace after the old King's death, the pornographers

and pamphleteers required a new focus—another woman who was interesting by virtue of her beauty, her proximity to the King, and the scandal she created by flouting courtly convention. Marie Antoinette fit the bill. And since most people outside the palace knew nothing whatsoever about the Queen save what they read in this 18th century version of the supermarket tabloid press, it soon ceased to matter what the truth of her life was. "In the midst of the financial crisis," writes one historian, "she was blamed for all the kingdom's woes. Her expenditures were denounced as the bottomless well that had absorbed the public resources." It was easy to believe that the woman in the pamphlets, licentious, unfeeling, unnatural, could be guilty of any degree of self-indulgence, even if it was ruining the national economy. Her new nickname, "Madame Deficit", reflected the public feeling.

Marie Antoinette had the misfortune to have been educated according to the old rules and expectations for royalty, only to find herself reigning in a new world—a world that was, for the first time, beginning to reject the very concept of monarchy. The age of the

Enlightenment had dawned; the American colonies had, by 1783, won their independence from England and founded a republic by the people, for the people. The French government had, since ancient times, acknowledged the existence of the "three estates"— the nobility, the clergy, and the common people—but the notion that "the people" constituted a political entity with inherent rights, existing in a state of contract with a government that could be charged with failure to live up to its duties, was entirely new.

Eighteenth century political philosophy was born out of the European race to colonize the New World. For the first time in a thousand years, there were new lands to populate, to Christianize, lands that enabled the European powers to drastically expand the borders of their empires without having to conquer and subdue their own neighbors. The economic opportunities that developed out of this expansion into the New World were making it possible for the poor to grow rich, or at least rich enough to own land. Since status, in Europe, was defined almost entirely by how much land one owned, how fertile that land was, and how many peasants had to pay you for the privilege of working it, the landowners in the colonies saw themselves as being a new kind of citizen, distinct from their forebears who had been dependent on the aristocratic class for their livelihood. Why should ordinary people continue to hold the landed classes in reverence, when land could now be had for the taking on the far side of the Atlantic? Why should they cripple themselves paying taxes to a government that did nothing to relieve their suffering? Such questions had always been asked, but now they were being asked by more people, at a volume that was increasingly difficult to ignore.

The image of Marie Antoinette which still persists today in pop culture can be summarized by the quote famously misattributed to her: after being told that the peasants had no bread to eat, she is supposed to have replied, with a flippancy and indifference that revealed her total lack of compassion for the suffering of her people, "Let them eat cake". In truth, she never made any such statement. Before Marie Antoinette was even born, that statement had been attributed to other queens, in other countries, in other political contexts. It was, in short, an urban legend, even in the 1780s. After she became Queen, Marie Antoinette soon learned that the people of France were poor, that they were suffering, and she was anything but indifferent to their plight. When she was married, she insisted that the royal processions steer around the cornfields, rather than trampling the peasants' livelihood under the wheels of the royal carriages. She made frequent large donations to charity. On New Years Day, 1784, when her daughter Marie Therese was six years old, Marie Antoinette brought a few toys to her chamber, and explained that there would be no presents this year: "I should have liked to have given you all these as New Year's gifts, but the winter is very hard, there is a crowd of unhappy people who have no bread to eat, no clothes to wear, no wood to make a fire. I have given them all my money; I have none left to buy you presents, so there will be none this year."

Not only did Marie Antoinette care for the suffering of the poor, but she was determined that her children would grow up in a more "natural" manner than previous princes and princesses of France. She exposed them to the company of children their own age who were inferior to them in rank. Whereas in former ages, a King's children were expected to live the same public-facing lifestyle, devoid of all privacy, as the King and Queen themselves, Marie Antoinette limited their exposure to the court and tried to give them what would today be called a "normal" upbringing. A contemporary comparison can be found in the upbringing of Britain's Prince William and Prince Harry, whose mother, Diana, Princess of Wales, determined that they should attend school with other children their age rather than being educated in the palace by a governess, as their father Prince Charles had been. But in the 18th century, this decision was seen as anything but normal. Her "disappearances" from the court—most often to her refuge of Petit Trianon, where no one came except at her express invitation—should have shown the public that she was a human being just like them, a mother devoted to private family life. Instead, it made her seem distant and unknowable. Thus a vacuum was created, which the pamphleteers filled with titillating misinformation and outright falsehoods.

La Petit Trianon

Petit Trianon, the private retreat where Marie Antoinette abandoned her three-foot tall hairdos for simple white muslin gowns and straw hats, was a whimsical world of rustic family. The main chateau had been built as a gift for the most famous mistress of Louis XIV, Madame du Pompadour, though she had died four years before it was completed. Under Marie Antoinette's supervision, Petit Trianon became, essentially, a farm, but it was a farm with all the dirt scrubbed off—a place where the Queen, in her spotless white muslin, could gather eggs in a basket for her own breakfast table and even milk a cow if she took a fancy to do so. The legend of Marie Antoinette as an out of touch Queen who played luxurious games of make-believe in which she was a simple dairy maid, while actual peasants were starving just a few miles outside the gates of the palace, stems from the fact that she increasingly preferred to spend her time at Petit Trianon with her children and closest friends. The image of the Queen in her straw bonnets, playing at farm labor, fit neatly with the persona of the "let them eat cake" Queen that existed only in people's imaginations.

Since the Queen was supposed to live her life in public, a spectacle for the consumption of others, the real scandal of Petit Trianon was not the expense; from the point of view of the court of Versailles, Petit Trianon was rife for mockery simply because the courtiers were not allowed to go there. Not even the King made appearances there unless the Queen had expressly invited him. But one of her regular invited guests was the Swedish count Axel von Fersen, a handsome courtier with whom the Queen had been close for several years. It was assumed that Marie Antoinette and Fersen were lovers. In fact, no evidence has ever been discovered that Marie Antoinette ever took lovers, but the fact that Count Fersen was in her immediate orbit, while the King kept his distance, was all the proof that people needed to be certain they were guilty of infidelity.

According to her close companion, Madame Campan, the Queen was sometimes importuned by men who fancied themselves candidates for the position of her lover, but she knew how to deal with them. After the Baron du Besenval came to her on his knees, making a grand declaration of his love, Marie Antoinette summoned Campan as witness:

"Her majesty, after having enjoined me to the strictest secrecy upon what she was about to impart, informed me, that finding herself alone with the baron, he began to address her with so much gallantry, that she was thrown into the utmost astonishment, and that he was mad enough to fall upon his knees, and make her a declaration in form. The Queen added, that she said to him: "Rise, sir: the King shall not be informed of an offence which would disgrace you for ever"; that the baron grew pale, and stammered an apology; that she left her closet without saying another word, and that since that time, she hardly ever spoke to him. The Queen said to me on this occasion: " It is delightful to have friends; but in a situation like mine, it is some times difficult to adopt the friends of our friends."

Marie Antoinette's reputation might have benefited had she chosen to humiliate Besenval in public instead of in private. But since she resolutely continued to look upon her private affairs as her own, people were allowed to persist in the assumption that she used that privacy to conduct debauched affairs, neglect her children, and amuse herself at the expense, and to the injury, of the nation.

As more and more peasants lost their land due to skyrocketing taxes, Marie Antoinette's Petit Trianon became a visible symbol of royal decadence. Even its remoteness from the main palace of Versailles was seen as being symbolic of how remote and uncaring the Queen was. In the words of one historian, she was seen as failing at "the basic duties expected of her as Queen". By now, the pamphlets depicting her as a sexually insatiable foreigner who made a mockery of her husband and all of France were so numerous, and so vile, that the King attempted to take measures to repress them. But the public appetite for the pamphlets was so strong that nothing could be done—most were not printed in France, anyway, but written and published overseas, then imported into the country. The Queen, as always, felt that the only proper, dignified response she could make was to ignore the problem entirely and act as though the pamphlets did not exist.

"Come and weep with me"

In 1772, Louis XV had commissioned a gift of jewelry for his mistress, the Comtesse du Barry. He specified that the Parisian jewelers Boehmer and Bassenge were to create a diamond necklace such as had never been seen before, for the astronomical price of two million livres (the modern equivalent of about fourteen million U.S. dollars). It would take several years for the jewelers to amass so large a set of matching diamonds, and they nearly went bankrupt in the process—but the King would make good all their expenses, and the jewelers would enjoy all the fame and prestige that would arise from having crafted such a unique masterpiece for the King's favorite. The King, however, caught smallpox and died before he could pay for the necklace, and the

Comtesse du Barry was exiled from court, never again to receive the extravagant gifts of the French king.

To describe the necklace as such is to create a misleading idea of its appearance. It was not a diamond pendant, or even a chain of diamonds. It stretched from shoulder to shoulder, with festoons, pendants, and tassels that draped over the breast and met in a point near the navel. To call it extravagant scarcely does it justice. It was practically jeweled armor.

There are conflicting reports as to what happened when Boehmer approached Louis, after the death of the old King, regarding the fate of the necklace. According to one account, Louis offered to purchase it for his new young Queen, but Marie Antoinette refused the gift, saying that such an enormous sum would be better spent outfitting a battleship. Other accounts claimed that the Queen refused to have a necklace, however gorgeous, which had originally been intended for someone as disreputable and low born as Madame du Barry. Still others claim that Louis initially meant to purchase the necklace for the Queen, only to change his mind on his own. In any event, Marie Antoinette never made any attempt to obtain the necklace for herself.

Marie Antoinette did purchase a set of diamond earrings from Boehmer, shortly after Louis became King. But she paid for the earrings, which cost about sixty thousand livres, out of her own privy purse, in monthly installments over several years. Perhaps for this reason, or perhaps out of sheer desperation to recover his losses, Boehmer, in 1785, became the dupe of a confidence artist who inveigled him into believing that the Queen had changed her mind about purchasing the necklace; and that, owing to its stupendous cost, and her fear of being seen as extravagant, she had chosen to act through an intermediary in order to obtain it. "Having seen that the young Queen took so much time to discharge, out of her savings, a debt she had contracted for an article that had tempted her, and which she did not like to make the public money pay for, Boehmer ought never to have lent himself to the belief, that eight or ten years afterwards, she would, without the King's knowledge, have purchased an ornament at fifteen hundred thousand livres," Madam Campan writes. "But the desire to dispose of so expensive an article as the famous necklace, the history of which is so generally, and at the same time so imperfectly known, and the hope of being paid in some way or other, induced him to believe that which he ought not to have thought even probable."

The deception surrounding the purchase of the necklace happened thus: there was a certain Cardinal de Rohan who had, during Maria Teresa's lifetime, been the French ambassador to the court of Vienna. Since the Empress's death and his return to France, he had fallen into disfavor at the court of Versailles, principally because Marie Antoinette was outraged over the gossip he had repeated to her mother regarding her "frivolous" behavior in France, and because she had discovered a letter he had written which referred to Maria Teresa in less than flattering terms. By August of 1784, Rohan had begun to cherish hopes that the Queen had forgotten her anger with him, and that he might manage to obtain appointment to some high office from the King. It was around this point that he made the acquaintance of a woman called Jeanne de la Motte, who became his mistress.

Cardinal de Rohan thought it worth his while to cultivate Jeanne de la Motte because she claimed, with so much boldness that it seemed impossible that she should be lying, to be on extremely intimate terms with the Queen. In fact, she had never spoken with the Queen, and had only managed to finagle entry to Versailles on the arm of one of her temporary lovers. But Rohan found la Motte's claims of friendship with the Queen convincing, and initiated a relationship with her for the express purpose of using her to win favor with Marie Antoinette. La Motte assured Rohan that she was doing everything in her power to make the Queen think well of him. Eventually, la Motte began to give Rohan letters, claiming they had been written by the Queen. In warm tones, these letters promised that Marie Antoinette was ready to put aside her previous bad feelings for him. Rohan's replies were entrusted to la Motte, who promised to pass them along to the

Queen. Before long, Rohan's correspondent claimed that she had fallen in love with him, and la Motte, still purporting to be deep in the Queen's confidence, affirmed to him that Marie Antoinette was besotted with him.

La Motte added the crowning touch to her deception in August of 1784, after Rohan implored her to arrange for him to meet with the Queen face to face—a meeting which should have been impossible for la Motte to arrange, if she were not truly as close to the Queen as she claimed to be. However, it had been many years since Rohan had spent much time in Marie Antoinette's presence, and in an age before television would make the faces of famous persons as familiar to strangers as the faces of their own family members, it was relatively easy for la Motte to find a substitute to play the role of the Queen. She hired a prostitute called Nicole Leguay, who bore a resemblance to Marie Antoinette, dressed her in a fine gown and jewels, and dispatched her to meet with Rohan in the gardens of Versailles under cover of darkness. Rohan offered the false Marie Antoinette the gift of a rose, a pledge of his love. Nicole Leguay, coached by la Motte, promised to use her position as Queen to do Rohan good.

Backed by this seemingly incontrovertible proof that la Motte was indeed highly placed in the Queen's confidence, Rohan began allowing her to "borrow" large sums of money in the Queen's name, ostensibly for her favorite charitable causes. In reality, of course, la Motte was pocketing the sums herself, using them to purchase clothes, jewels, and other trappings that would enhance her status at court and reinforce the ruse that she was a highborn aristocrat of the Queen's inner circle. Eventually, la Motte's reputation for being an approachable royal insider attracted the attention of the jewelers Boehmer and Bassenge. Boehmer offered la Motte a commission on the sale if she could persuade the Queen to purchase the necklace from them.

Instantly, la Motte sensed an opportunity to make an astronomical amount of money. In late January of 1785, she approached Rohan, telling him that the Queen wished to buy Boehmer's necklace, but that she did not have enough money of her own to purchase it. She didn't dare allow it to be known that she wished to use public funds in order to obtain such an extravagant piece of jewelry for herself, not when the French people were already suffering under such economic hardship. The only way she could get the necklace was by borrowing the money from a private individual who would keep her secrets for her; the Queen would be sure to repay the loan over time, not only with gold, but with her increasing favor and affection. The letter which begged this favor of Rohan was signed "Marie Antoinette de France." Neither la Motte, nor, apparently, Rohan, knew that the Kings and Queens of France signed letters with their Christian name only. (The signature "Marie Antoinette" was thus the equivalent of the style "Elizabeth R.", used by English monarchs.)

In the belief that he was cementing his place in the Queen's affections, Rohan approached Boehmer and showed him the letters purporting to be from Marie Antoinette. He bargained terms with Boehmer, agreeing that the necklace would be purchased for 2,000,000 *livres*; Boehmer gave the necklace into

Rohan's keeping, and Rohan took it directly to the home of Jeanne de la Motte. In Rohan's presence, la Motte gave the necklace to a man whom she claimed served the Queen as a valet. He would, she assured the Cardinal, convey the necklace directly to Marie Antoinette. Instead, the necklace was conveyed to la Motte's husband, who took it to London, where it was broken into pieces, that the diamonds might each be sold separately.

When the time came to pay the jeweler, Jeanne la Motte produced the notes Rohan had given her, guaranteeing the price of the necklace. But Boehmer did not want notes; he wanted money. When no money was forthcoming, he went directly to the Queen to complain. Marie Antoinette told him that she had never given any orders for the necklace to be purchased. Boehmer explained to her that he had negotiated with her emissaries, the Cardinal de Rohan and her intimate friend, Jeanne la Motte. Since Marie Antoinette had never heard of la Motte, it was immediately apparent that a tremendous crime had been committed in the Queen's name.

In August of 1785, a trial of sorts commenced. It was the feast day of the Assumption of Mary, an important holiday in the church calendar, and the entire court of Versailles was assembled to accompany the King and Queen to the chapel for services. Cardinal de Rohan was supposed to officiate the Mass; instead, he was ordered to appear before the King, the Queen, the Minister of the Courts, and the Keeper of the Seals, to explain how he had come to promise two million *livres* in the Queen's name. In his defense, Rohan produced a letter bearing the signature *Marie Antoinette de France.* Louis was incensed; Rohan was of aristocratic birth, and he knew perfectly well that the Queen's signature was simply *Marie Antoinette.* Either he was lying about being duped, or he was blinded by greed and by love for the King's wife. Either way, the King was furious. He ordered the Cardinal arrested and taken to the Bastille. Three days later—long after she had received sufficient warning to burn all of her papers—Jeanne la Motte was arrested, along with Nicole Leguay and the forger, Rétaux de Villette, who had written all of the letters purporting to be from the Queen.

Rohan and his accomplices were brought to trial before the Parlement de Paris, despite the fact that Pope Pius VI claimed the right to try the Cardinal himself. The *parlement* was not a parliament in the modern sense of the word, meaning a legislative body, but rather an assembly of appellate judges. The Parlement was one of the only institutions of French government whose power did not derive from the King. As one historian puts it, the Parlement de Paris was "a small, selfish, proud and venal oligarchy, [which] regarded itself, and was regarded by public opinion, as the guardian of the constitutional liberties of France." In other words, it did not represent the rights of the common people, but it did represent the rights of the aristocracy, as a class distinct from royalty. The Parlement returned not guilty verdicts in the cases of Rohan and the prostate Nicole Leguay; the forger Villette was banished. Jeanne de la Motte was ordered to be beaten with a whip, after which she was branded on each shoulder with the letter V for *voleuse,* meaning thief; afterwards, she was consigned to a prison for prostitutes.

Marie Antoinette regarded Rohan's acquittal as a slap in the face—which was the intended effect. "Come and weep with me," she wrote to one of her friends. "The judgement that has just been pronounced is a grievous insult." The message was clear: the only grounds on which Rohan could have been acquitted of all blame was if the judges of the Parlement de Paris considered it perfectly reasonable for a man of his stature to suppose that the Queen was selfish enough to covet the necklace at public expense, deceptive enough to do it behind the King's back, and immoral enough to conduct an affair with a Cardinal of the Church in order to obtain her goal. For so many years, she had tried to turn a blind eye to the libels that were printed against her. Only now, when it was too late, had she discovered the damage the pamphleteers had done to her reputation. The people of France, including the judges of the Parlement, believed her to be, in truth, the debauched, unfeeling Queen that appeared between the pages of the pamphlets. It was a crushing realization.

This was to be the great turning point of Marie Antoinette's life—the moment at which her charmed, glittering royal existence began to slide inexorably down the path that led to the Revolution, the guillotine, and the destruction of the *ancien régime*. The court which had acquitted Rohan had condemned her. In the hearts and minds of the people, it was she, not la Motte, not Rohan, who was the villain of the "diamond necklace affair", as it came to be called. Now, it was not merely pornographic pamphlets which dragged the Queen's name through the mud. Pens all over Europe were busily scratching over parchment, including that of Jeanne de la Motte—disguised as a boy, she escaped from prison shortly after she was confined, and went on to write a pamphlet of her own, *Memoires Justificatifs de La Comtesse de Valois de La Motte*, which, according to Madam Campan, did more harm to the Queen's reputation than almost anything else printed against her. Published in 1789, the same year that the Bastille was stormed, it contains this sentimental indictment against that prison, where la Motte was held for a short time before her trial:

"...At this moment I am going to strike the reader with horror against a government, which all the universe has long supposed to be renowned for wisdom and justice. In the following assertions, so far from being suspected of exceeding, I may possibly be censured for falling short of the truth. Is it for imagination to conceive, is it for the most vivid colors of description to blazon adequately, the horrors of that dreadful Bastille? I shudder even at the very name of that dungeon of despair, that tomb of broken hearts, where so many miserable victims have been immured, without any accusation, without even being acquainted with the nature of their offence, but doomed by the arbitrary will of the Sovereign to pine away their miserable existence, till Death, dreadful as he is to others, (basking in the sun shine of prosperity, and reveling in one continued round of fashionable amusements) wears here a very different aspect: here he appears like a smiling angel, a kind deliverer, whose approach they anticipate with rapture, whose touch dissolves their fetters. Ye horrid towers! dire monuments of despotism! disgrace of human nature, are ye then fallen at last? Your dungeons have disgorged their victims, and, thanks to Liberty, ye are levelled in the dust! As innocent prisoner in your gloomy caves, these eyes have beheld your terrors, the reflection of which creates such a depression of spirits, as nothing can equal but the joy of my heart, in contemplating your destruction!"

The press began to paint Marie Antoinette as a Queen who would do anything to gratify her perverse desires. She was said to be maddened by sexual frenzy. A phrase was coined—"a fury in the uterus"— to describe this condition. Even amongst those who were capable of recognizing that most of what was printed about Marie Antoinette was nothing more than salacious scandalmongering, there persisted a belief that she had intentionally duped and disgraced Cardinal de Rohan, merely because she disliked him.

With every new assault that was mounted against Marie Antoinette, the security of her husband's throne began to crumble. If the Queen's vices could not be checked by the King, then he was no fit king at all. After all, a man who could not rule his wife could not be expected to rule a country. Even in the Enlightenment, the so-called Age of Reason, this was considered nothing less than immutable, unquestionable truth.

Chapter Five: Her Mother's Daughter

The beginning of the end

In 1787, Marie Antoinette posed, with her four children, for a simple, domestic family portrait, in which the figures were deliberately arranged in order to invoke the Holy Family. In this portrait, she wears a fairly simple red gown, which, in accordance with the fashions of the time, places her bosom on ample display. The display is not provocative, however; her low-cut neckline draws attention to nothing, save an expanse of bare skin. She is wearing a pair of earrings, but conspicuously, she wears no necklace. The portrait was an attempt to salvage her image. "Here is the Queen as she in truth," it pleads. "A noble lady, a modest woman, a devoted mother." The portrait was not the end of it; in a sincere, if belated, attempt to alter public perception of her, she changed her ways. Her private dressmaker was sent away, the gambling tables removed from her chambers, and all her personal expenses pared down to the bone.

At last, she had learned the lesson that Maria Teresa had been trying to impart to her practically since the moment she set foot in France. It would prove too late to be her salvation; but at the same time, the crisis brought out the best in her nature. Within six years, Marie Antoinette, Louis, and all of their children save for Marie Therese, the eldest, would be dead. But during those six years, Marie Antoinette accomplished something her mother had despaired of her ever achieving. She became a true Queen, well-informed, conversant in the political issues of the day. And in a very real sense, she was briefly the ruler of France. Louis XVI, who had never been as resolute as his wife, had a nervous breakdown in 1787 and spent all his time in Marie Antoinette's rooms, weeping. With the King so indisposed, the Queen began to attend meetings of his royal council. She was, admittedly, at a considerable disadvantage when she attempted to act in the King's executive capacity. The deficits of her education had never been more important, nor more obvious. She knew, from observation, that the people of France were suffering, but she knew very little about the particulars of governmental administration that had produced those conditions. She knew nothing about French government or French history. As a result, the council meetings over which she presided were somewhat disorganized. "Her majesty now seems entirely occupied with discussions of economies and reforms," observed on foreign minister, "but all these affairs are treated without any method or prearranged plan and the result is a confusion which aggravates the evil instead of lessening it." Rather than regarding her widening political role in a favorable light, as a wife's attempt to lessen her husband's burdens, people began to claim, once again, that she was an Austrian agent, promoting the interests of her homeland over the interests of France.

The Third Estate

When Louis recovered his composure, he found that a significant number of his own nobles were now in favor of launching a comprehensive campaign of financial reform that would lessen the suffering of the people after yet another poor harvest and terrible winter. Reluctantly, the King convened the Estates General, an ancient semi-parliamentary body representing the "three estates" of France: the nobility, the clergy, and commoners. This was the first time the estates had been called since 1614, and the move signaled the King's desperation to retain some degree of control over the rapidly foundering ship of state. "These gentlemen wish to restrain the power of the King," remarked Marie Antoinette, with some foresight, "but they will bring about their own destruction." In his *Lettre du Roi,* Louis ordered that the "most notable persons" of each community and judicial district should convene in Paris in order to "to confer and to record remonstrances, complaints, and grievances" against the general state of affairs in the realm. Of the three estates, the People, or the Commons, was naturally the largest, but in the past, the Nobles and the Clergy had commanded a two-to-one voting majority against them. During the Estates General of 1789, however, the people began to insist that each delegate have but a single vote, which would ensure majority rule. With some misgiving, Louis agreed to this measure. There were about 100 members of the Clergy, 400 members of the Nobles, and 578 men representing the Third Estate. Louis and Marie Antoinette clung to the hope that most of the nobility and the clergy were still on their side.

Calling the Estates General at all had been a devastating move on the King's part. France had no permanent parliamentary body, nor a written constitution. The constitution of France was held to reside in the monarchy itself, and parliament, such as it was, consisted of the King holding counsel with his ministers. The power of the French king had always been absolute and both Louis and Marie Antoinette sensed that by sharing executive power with the delegates of the three estates, they were weakening the monarchy forever. They could only hope that the Nobles and the Clergy would recognize that they stood to lose more power to the Commons than they stood to take away from the King. But the decision did not long remain in their hands. In June of 1789, the Third Estate separated from the Estates General and reformed as the National Assembly—an assembly of the common people, or *Communes*, as they would come to be known during the Revolution. The National Assembly invited the nobility and the clergy to join them, but made it clear that, with or without their cooperation, they intended to produce a written national constitution.

On June 4, 1789, the Dauphin, Louis Joseph, Marie Antoinette's second child, died of tuberculosis. There were few signs that the public mourned him at all, or even noticed his passing. The Queen was heartbroken, not merely by the loss of her second child—two years before, her younger daughter had also died, when she was only 11 months old—but by the dawning awareness that her family had entirely lost the love of their people. "At the death of my poor little prince, the people hardly seemed to notice," she wrote. Louis Joseph's suffering was long and terrible, and the King and Queen were too distracted to pay the necessary attention to the political crisis that was about to engulf them.

Not all the delegates of the Third Estate were peasants. Certain aristocrats and clergymen who were known to be advocates for the poor had been chosen by the people of their districts to serve as delegates for the Communes by right of election. These aristocrats and clergy served as liaisons to the King, and worked tirelessly to convince him that giving his assent to a written constitution would be the best thing he could do, both for himself and for France. Louis could not easily come to a decision. He was being asked to do something that no French king had ever been asked to do before—there were few historical precedents for converting an absolute monarchy into a constitutional monarchy, at least not in recent history. "The King [was] of two minds," observes one historian, "the Queen [was] of one mind." Marie Antoinette, convinced of the necessity of preserving the absolute power of the monarchy, persuaded Louis to surround Paris with troops loyal to the crown, where they would be in a position to occupy the capital and shut the National Assembly down. This decision—threatening the delegates with military reprisal—would prove to be the spark that ignited the tinderbox of the French Revolution.

It is at this point that the genuine tragedy of Marie Antoinette's poor education begins to be truly felt. In Russia, only two decades earlier, Catherine the Great, a devoted student of Enlightenment philosophy, had of her own volition convened a national assembly, representing every class of person living in Russia, and presented them with her *Nakaz,* or "Instructions". The purpose of the assembly was to overhaul Russia's ancient, crumbling legal code, but since Russian history had no precedent for any form of self-government, Catherine had drafted the *Nakaz* and instructed that it be read aloud to the assembly, in the hopes that it would teach the people how to be self-governing. The assembly made little progress in effecting legal reform in Russia, but the case demonstrates the intellectual flexibility with which a highly educated, forward-thinking sovereign could confront the problems facing her government. Had Marie Antoinette shared Catherine's bookish nature, or had she, like Catherine, been confined for long periods early in her marriage with no means of amusing herself save with books, would she have feared the power of the people less? Would she have guarded the King's absolute power so jealously, even after it became apparent that the people of France, once united against him, were capable of destroying him? History is full of these question marks. Having no such education to guide and inform her, Marie Antoinette did what came naturally to her. Remembering the iron will of her mother, the Empress, she encouraged Louis to order the doors of the National Assembly's meeting place shut and barred.[1] It did not seem to occur to her that the delegates were determined enough to simply pack up and move to a different location to continue their constitutional deliberations. But that is precisely what they did.

Revolution

---

[1] Regarding Catherine the Great, it is worth noting that, despite her high Enlightenment ideals, she was hugely upset by the French Revolution and the executions of Louis and Marie Antoinette. It is said that she destroyed a bust of George Washington which adorned her study, as though blaming the man she had once so admired for opening the door to bloody revolution in Europe.

The Bastille only contained seven prisoners when it was stormed and liberated on July 14, 1789. Though the famous French prison was considered a notorious symbol of the King's autocratic power, being a place where prisoners could be detained indefinitely without charge, none of the prisoners then incarcerated were the true object of the liberation. Earlier, revolutionaries loyal to the National Assembly had stolen 28,000 muskets; they now needed the Bastille's huge stores of gunpowder in order to make use of them. Paris was only about ten miles away from Versailles, but still, the news did not reach the King until it was too late to order a military intervention.

On July 14th, Louis went to bed at 10 in the evening; it was strictly against palace decorum to disturb him until after dawn the next day. But at two in the morning on July the 15th, he was awakened by the Master of the Wardrobe and informed that the Bastille had been taken, its governor beheaded, and his head paraded on a pike through the streets of Paris by an angry mob. "Is it a revolt?" the King asked. "No, sire," came the reply. "It is a revolution." Versailles, which had been tranquil all the day before, erupted into a state of general panic. The majority of the courtiers deserted the palace. Marie Antoinette wished to flee as well, to a small town near the Austrian border, where her brother Leopold, who had become Emperor after the death of her brother Joseph in 1790, would be able to send Austrian troops to protect them. Louis, however, refused to leave; the people were attempting to strip him of throne, but he would not leave that throne empty, not of his own free will. Marie Antoinette feared for their lives, but she would not leave Louis's side. "I am shaken by this succession of blows," wrote the Queen to a friend. "We are surrounded by hardships and misfortunes. But you may be sure that adversity has not lessened my strength or my courage."

Within a bare few weeks, the old social order in France had broken down completely. The National Assembly, true to Marie Antoinette's prediction, declared that the aristocracy and the clergy were stripped of their feudal privilege, that the serfs were liberated, and that the Assembly would not dissolve until a constitution had been resolved upon. The body proclaimed the Declaration of the Rights of Man, which was drafted with considerable input by Thomas Jefferson and the Marquis de la Fayette, a French nobleman who had become a hero of the American Revolution. The Declaration, consisting of seventeen articles, derived from Enlightenment philosophy and struck directly at the heart of the King's ancient authority by investing the people with inherent rights which could not be countermanded by royal privilege:

Article I – Men are born and remain free and equal in rights. Social distinctions can be founded only on the common good.

Article II – The goal of any political association is the conservation of the natural and imprescriptible rights of man. These rights are liberty, property, safety and resistance against oppression.

Article III – The principle of any sovereignty resides essentially in the Nation. No body, no individual can exert authority which does not emanate expressly from it.

Article IV – Liberty consists of doing anything which does not harm others: thus, the exercise of the natural rights of each man has only those borders which assure other members of the society the fruition of these same rights. These borders can be determined only by the law.

Article V – The law has the right to forbid only actions harmful to society. Anything which is not forbidden by the law cannot be impeded, and no one can be constrained to do what it does not order.

Article VI – The law is the expression of the general will. All the citizens have the right of contributing personally or through their representatives to its formation. It must be the same for all, either that it protects, or that it punishes. All the citizens, being equal in its eyes, are equally admissible to all public dignities, places, and employments, according to their capacity and without distinction other than that of their virtues and of their talents.

Article VII – No man can be accused, arrested nor detained but in the cases determined by the law, and according to the forms which it has prescribed. Those who solicit, dispatch, carry out or cause to be carried out arbitrary orders, must be punished; but any citizen called or seized under the terms of the law must obey at once; he renders himself culpable by resistance.

Article VIII – The law should establish only penalties that are strictly and evidently necessary, and no one can be punished but under a law established and promulgated before the offense and legally applied.

Article IX – Any man being presumed innocent until he is declared culpable if it is judged indispensable to arrest him, any rigor which would not be necessary for the securing of his person must be severely reprimanded by the law.

Article X – No one may be disturbed for his opinions, even religious ones, provided that their manifestation does not trouble the public order established by the law.

Article XI – The free communication of thoughts and of opinions is one of the most precious rights of man: any citizen thus may speak, write, print freely, except to respond to the abuse of this liberty, in the cases determined by the law.

Article XII – The guarantee of the rights of man and of the citizen necessitates a public force: this force is thus instituted for the advantage of all and not for the particular utility of those in whom it is trusted.

Article XIII – For the maintenance of the public force and for the expenditures of administration, a common contribution is indispensable; it must be equally distributed to all the citizens, according to their ability to pay.

Article XIV – Each citizen has the right to ascertain, by himself or through his representatives, the need for a public tax, to consent to it freely, to know the uses to which it is put, and of determining the proportion, basis, collection, and duration.

Article XV – The society has the right of requesting an account from any public agent of its administration.

Article XVI – Any society in which the guarantee of rights is not assured, nor the separation of powers determined, has no Constitution.

Article XVII – Property being an inviolable and sacred right, no one can be deprived of private usage, if it is not when the public necessity, legally noted, evidently requires it, and under the condition of a just and prior indemnity.

The National Assembly likewise upheld freedom of the press, which meant that the royal censors, which had been employed overtime in checking the publication of the libelous, pornographic pamphlets written against the Queen, were no longer in a position to do so. Since the beginning, the subtext of the pamphlets was that Marie Antoinette was more powerful than her husband, a sexually insatiable dominatrix who led the King about by the nose. Now that the Queen was taking an active role in politics, fear of her power was elevated from subtext to text. If the King remained in power, the pamphlets and newspapers warned, it would really be *l'Autrichienne*, the foreigner, who would rule through him. The vitriol was fueled by the fact that the Queen had established herself as an enemy to the Revolution, and her political critics invoked the fear of "female rule" as a means of undermining the monarchy further. "The King has only one man on whom he can depend," said the revolutionaries. "And that is the Queen."

About three months after the Bastille was stormed, a mob comprised entirely of peasant women armed with sharpened broom handles and pitchforks marched on Versailles, demanding bread. Louis, who had thrown himself into hunting to distract himself from the chaos around him, was away from the palace when they arrived; Marie Antoinette was ensconced in her refuge at Petit Trianon, strolling through the gardens. As the women drew nearer, they began to speak of tearing the Queen limb from limb, one woman crying for her head, another for her entrails. They nearly accomplished their aims. By early the next morning, two guards had been killed, and the women had pushed their way into the palace; the guard's lives bought the Queen just enough time to slip out of her chambers through a secret exit before the women burst into her rooms. Furious at having been denied their prey, the women stabbed the Queen's bed through with their pikes. It was, essentially, a symbolic rape. A mob of commoners had violated the Queen's chambers, thus symbolically violating the aura of untouchability which surrounded the Queen herself, and by extension, the entire royal family. Marie Antoinette, Louis, and their household, were forced to leave Versailles that very afternoon. It was to be the last time they would ever see the palace. "We are lost, dragged away, perhaps to death," Marie Antoinette wrote. "When kings become prisoners they are very near it."

The King, Queen, Dauphin, and Madame Royale were taken to the palace of Tuileries, in Paris, where they were placed under guard by the National Assembly. They could not leave, and their communications were monitored. Marie Antoinette suffered a mental breakdown; she could think of nothing but the danger to her family, and the awful, incomprehensible degree to which she had lost the faith of the people of France. She suffered constant bouts of uncontrollable weeping; yet, even as death loomed nearer, the secret steel spine she had inherited from Maria Teresa became more and more evident. The King was virtually paralyzed, by now little more than a hapless bystander to events. In his place, Marie Antoinette began to assume the role of monarch. She, who had always loathed reading and could write only with labor and difficulty, learned how to write in a secret diplomatic cipher code so that she could communicate, in the King's name, with foreign ambassadors, in the hopes of securing military assistance from brother in Austria. "As far as we are personally concerned, happiness is over and done with, whatever the course of events may be," wrote the Queen, who was now just 34 years old. "If only what we are now suffering could be counted on to make our children happy. Tribulation first makes you realize who you are."

Restoring the monarchy to its previous power was a remote dream; there was only one goal that seemed attainable now. By day she met with ambassadors and advisors; in the evenings, she sewed large tapestries. By night, she began to hatch a to save the lives of the King and their two children.

Escape from Tuileries

There were a handful of nobles who supported the National Assembly, but remained personally sympathetic to and supportive of the King and Queen. One of these was Axel Fersen, the Swedish nobleman who had been such a frequent guest of the

Queen's at Petit Trianon. He could not afford to visit Marie Antoinette openly, but he came to see her in secret. Alarmed by the presence of so many of the National Guard at the palace, and convinced that the revolutionaries would not rest until they found some pretext to see her and Louis executed, Fersen offered to help Marie Antoinette and some of her household escape from the palace.

At midnight, on June 20, 1791, the King and Queen and their two children, along with three courtiers, boarded a carriage and set off from Tuileries. They were all in disguise; the Queen as a servant, the King as a fat, middle-aged baroness, their son Louis Charles as a little girl. The courtiers also traveled in the guise of servants. Axel Fersen was the carriage driver. It had fallen to Marie Antoinette to do all of the planning; Louis was terrified by the risks of an escape attempt, and kept insisting they change the date of the attempt. (They would have departed on the 19th, but Louis did not want to travel on a Sunday.) The most dangerous part of the escape, they thought, would be slipping out of Tuileries past the National Guard, but they would not be absolutely safe until they reached the end of their 200-mile journey and made for the safety of Austria, where Marie Antoinette trusted her brother to look after them. Everything was uncertain, and Louis's nervous constitution did not tolerate uncertainty well. But Marie Antoinette was resolute. "Our position is horrible," she wrote. "I have trusted in time and in the hope that public opinion would change. But today all is different. If we would escape destruction, we must take the only path open to us. If we must perish let us do so gloriously."

At first, it seemed as if the escape had been a success. Marie Antoinette began to relax after they had been on the road for a few hours, saying that, if they were going to have been caught, she thought it would have happened already. Their absence from the palace had not been discovered until the King's servants came to wake him at his customary hour in the morning, and at that point they had already been traveling for seven hours. Outside Paris, the party switched coaches. Despite the urgent need for speed and secrecy, the King and Queen had been unable to completely dispense with the almost superstitious need to observe royal etiquette, which required them to travel in a certain amount of luxury. As a result, the carriage was weighed down by such unnecessary items as tea sets and a toilet with a leather cover. Worst of all, the King had dismissed Axel Fersen, the only person in the party who had any real idea how to pull off a stealthy escape attempt. Louis was concerned that, because Fersen was Swedish, it would be said he had been liberated by the Swedish. With Fersen no longer driving the coach, which groaned under the weight of so many people and so much luggage, the royal party simply could not travel quickly enough to avoid detection. In Varennes, forty miles from the Austrian border, they were recognized by a former cavalry officer, who sounded the alarm.

A group of citizens loyal to the Revolution apprehended the King and his family, and they were returned to Paris—slowly, in a procession that lasted more than four days. The people of France were owed the opportunity to gaze upon the King and Queen in their disgrace; there was no better way to de-mystify the very concept of royalty than by parading Louis XVI and his family through the streets like a prisoner.

By definition, the king was a person who led a remote existence, shielded from the scrutiny and opinion of the commoners. No French king had ever been exposed to the jeering and shouting of angry mobs before; but if the King could be made to appear humble and inept before the very eyes of the people, then how was he any different from anyone else? And to set eyes on Marie Antoinette was to gaze upon a she-devil from a terrifying legend; when she attempted to give her food to the hungry peasants pressing up against the sides of the coach, people cried, "Don't touch it! It might be poisoned."

The escape from Tuileries placed the King and Queen in a far more dangerous position than they had been in before. Louis had left a declaration behind him, which was discovered and read in his absence; it described, in detail, his reasons for fleeing the country, which amounted to a list of complaints over the way he had been treated since he was made captive. It ended with a plaintive reminder to "all Frenchmen and above all Parisians" that, as King, he was "your father, your best friend." He expressed his hopes that he would soon be able to return to a

France which would present him with a constitution he could accept in good conscience—one in which the rights of "our ancient religion" were safeguarded. But it was also known, or at least suspected (for Marie Antoinette had been exceptionally careful to leave no evidence) that their real goal in making for Austria was to return again to Paris at the head of a column of Austrian soldiers—though Louis and Marie Antoinette both insisted under cross-examination that they had never intended to leave France. The Queen was depicted as a monster thirsting for the blood of her own people. She was, apparently, just French enough to be considered a traitor, though never French enough to escape the stigma of being foreign.

After being returned to Tuileries, it seemed at first to the King's friends that he was not in as much danger as had initially been feared. The dominant party in the National Assembly were not complete radicals— they held out hope that the needed government reforms could be carried out without abolishing the monarchy. It was said that the King and his family had been "abducted" from Tuileries, and safely returned by the National Guard. There were other elements in the Assembly that wanted nothing more than to see Louis XVI with his head on a pike, but the prevailing sentiment was that the great powers of Europe would only recognize the legitimacy of a constitutional government in France if it bore the legitimate King's imprimatur. However, the various parties of the Assembly were beginning to resort to violence between themselves to settle their political and ideological differences. The pro-monarchist party would not remain in the majority for much longer.

On September 3, 1791, the National Assembly presented the first written French constitution. It did not live up to Louis' hopes for a constitution that would respect the traditional role of Roman Catholicism in French law; it specifically stated that marriage would be considered a civil institution only. The constitution's final section, "Of Monarchy, the Regency, and the Ministers", charged the King with defending the very constitution which gutted the throne of real power:

"1.   Monarchy is indivisible, and is delegated hereditarily to the reigning family, from male to male, by order of primogeniture, to the perpetual exclusion of women and their descendants.

(Nothing is presumed concerning the effect of renunciations in the present reigning family.)

2.   The person of the King is inviolable and sacred; his only title is King of the French.

3.   There is no authority in France superior to that of the law; the King reigns only thereby, and only in the name of the law may he exact obedience.

4.   On his accession to the throne, or as soon as he has attained his majority, the King, in the presence of the legislative body, shall take oath to the nation to be faithful to the nation and to the law, to employ all the power delegated to him to maintain the Constitution decreed by the National Constituent Assembly in the years 1789, 1790, and 1791, and to have the laws executed.

If the legislative body be not in session, the King shall have a proclamation published, in which said oath, and the promise to reiterate it as soon as the legislative body has assembled, shall be set forth.

5. If, one month after the invitation of the legislative body, the King has not taken said oath, or if, after having taken it, he retracts it, he shall be deemed to have abdicated the throne.

6. If the King places himself at the head of an army and directs the forces thereof against the nation, or if he does not, by a formal statement, oppose any such undertaking carried on in his name, he shall be deemed to have abdicated the throne."

The last two items in the list seemed to be aimed at Marie Antoinette, or were at least inspired by her reputation for extravagance:

"9. The private property which the. King possesses upon his accession to the throne is irrevocably united with the national domain; he may dispose of property acquired by singular title; if he has not disposed thereof, it likewise is united at the end of the reign.

10. The nation provides for the splendor of the throne by a civil list, the sum of which shall be

determined by the legislative body at each change of reign, for the entire duration of the reign."

The Constitution of 1791—which would endure for only a year—was "a tissue of absurdities", in Marie Antoinette's opinion. Yet she was urged to accept it, and to use her influence to make the King accept it. A sympathetic delegate of the Assembly by the name of Barnave wrote to the Queen that she could be "still Queen of France but a far more beloved Queen than in the past. He told her that she had misunderstood the nature of the Revolution so far... It was true that the Queen had been the object of widespread resentment, but with her courage and character she could overcome this. The candour with which the Queen had always expressed her convictions...would now work to her advantage. If she openly supported the Constitution, she would be believed to be equally sincere." On September 14, "according to the wish of the great majority of the nation", Louis XVI proceeded to the Assembly to make his acceptance of the new Constitution public; he was provided, not with a throne, but with a simple chair on which a fleur-de-lis had been painted. The guards kept theirs hats on when he spoke.

The King's powers were greatly reduced, but not nonexistent. He could appoint ministers, had the power of veto over new laws, and though he could not declare war unilaterally, the Legislative Assembly could only declare war upon the King's request. On April 20, 1792, Louis was asked to request the Assembly to declare war on Austria. The crowned heads of Europe were already looking nervously at France, terrified that the disease of revolution and anarchy, which had germinated in the newly independent United States of America and erupted in a new, more terrifying form in Paris, would spread to other countries. This was precisely what some parties in the National Assembly wished for—to spread the anti-monarchist fervor to Austria and ignite a revolution there against the Emperor. Strangely enough, war with Austria was also the wish of Marie Antoinette. She was convinced that her brother Leopold would be swiftly victorious against the revolutionary forces and march into Paris in triumph to restore Louis to his former glory. The King agreed to ask for a declaration of war against Austria—then did not speak for the next ten days. Marie Antoinette told their friends that "He fears to give orders...he is crushed by an over-tender conscience." As for herself, "I would like to act, on horseback if necessary. But, if I acted so, it would give weapons to the King's enemies. The outcry against *l'autrichienne,* against the domination of a female, would be general in France. In showing myself, I would destroy the King."

Austria repelled the French attack in the spring, but the war would continue for another twenty-three years. From Tuileries, Marie Antoinette became, at last in truth, the spy she had been accused of being since her arrival in France. She kept her eyes and ears open, and passed as much information about French military movements as she could learn to her brother Leopold in Austria. She was not treacherous by nature, but the Revolution had forced her into the role of a traitor. Preserving the monarchy was her sole concern—and if she had to commit treason to accomplish, then so be it.

Arrest of Louis XVI

On June 20, 1792, a year to the day since the failed escaped attempt from Tuileries, "a mob of terrifying aspect" was permitted to enter the palace grounds by the National Guard, who recently been put in the place of the King's usual loyal bodyguards. They carried the traditional weapons of an angry mob—pitchforks, pikes, kitchen knives—as well as more gruesome articles, such as a doll hanging from a stick, which was proclaimed to be an effigy of Marie Antoinette hanging by the neck from a lamp post. With shouts of "Tyrant, tyrant!" they demanded to be ushered into the King's presence. But Louis behaved well; his ponderous nature, which made him so slow to act, allowed him to absorb this terrifying spectacle with relative composure. He was offered the *bonnet rouge*, the symbol of the Revolution, to wear, and he accepted it graciously, though it was too small to fit on his large head. He also drank a toast to the people of France. Marie Antoinette had insisted, at first, on being by the King's side when the people forced their way into his presence, but she was warned that if the people caught sight of her, the King would be in even more danger. Instead, she hid in a secret compartment in Louis Charles's rooms with her son and daughter. After the mob had gone, all three rushed out to embrace the King. His life had been in danger, and they all knew it. But the danger was only increasing.

A few weeks later, in early August, a mob of ten thousand people stormed the palace of Tuileries. The guards who had been charged with the King and Queen's safety begged them to come to the National Assembly and accept its protection—which is another way of saying that they would be prisoners. The Queen wanted to stay, but was persuaded to go when it was pointed out to her that all of her friends and faithful servants would be killed if she were found inside the palace when the mob broke in. The King likewise wished to stay, but he had made a tour of the palace's defenses earlier in the day, and found himself being openly jeered by the National Guard; it would be foolish, he realized, to expect them to protect his family from the mob. Surrounded by a few loyal guards and companions, Marie Antoinette,

Louis, and their two children were led out of the palace. Louis Joseph, almost eleven, was the only member of his family who did not seem to feel the danger; he kicked at a pile of leaves, sending them fluttering up into the air. "What a lot of leaves," remarked the King. "They have fallen early this year."

The National Assembly now had to decide what was to become of Louis XVI, his Queen, his heir, and his daughter. They could not be returned to Tuileries under additional protection because the mob, bursting in after their departure, had rendered the palace uninhabitable. This was especially unfortunate because the Queen had anticipated they would return to the palace relatively soon, so no one had packed any personal possessions. They were given a small suite of rooms at the Convent of the Feuillants, which had been the original meeting place of the pro-monarchist party of the National Assembly. A few days later, on August 13th, they were moved to even sparser accommodations in the Tower at the Square du Temple; rather like the Tower of London, the Tower in Temple Square had both squalid and luxurious quarters, and was used to host honored guests as well as confine prisoners. While their needs were provided for, there was no room for the usual royal complement of servants and retainers. Louis, Marie Antoinette, Louis's sister Madame Elisabeth, and the two children were permitted nine retainers, close friends who had been with them for many years—but only after Louis pointed out that Charles I, who had been executed during the English Civil War, had been allowed to keep his friends near him until the day he mounted the scaffold.

For about a week, the group lived like an ordinary family—educating and caring for the children, keeping each other's spirits up. But they were poised on the brink of something too monstrous to fathom, let alone anticipate. August of 1792, the month of their imprisonment, also saw the introduction of the guillotine in Paris. The guillotine had been designed by its creator as a humane, scientific instrument of execution, rendering the victim dead before they could register the slightest sensation of shock or pain. Compared to the former method of beheading, in which an inept headsman might take two or three blows to separate a person's head from their shoulders, the guillotine certainly involved less physical suffering. But it evoked little peace of mind amongst the victims of the Reign of Terror, the two-year period of the Revolution during which the guillotine began "working overtime on France's enemies". The Terror began with the September Massacre, during which several of Louis and Marie Antoinette's friends were seized, cross-examined, then brutally killed. Marie Antoinette's closest friend, the Princess de Lamballe, who had been with her since her marriage, was murdered, her head paraded through the streets on a pike. The mob gathered outside the royal chambers in the Tower and thrust the pike up before the windows, demanding that the Queen kiss her friend goodbye. Marie Antoinette rose to see, but she fainted before she actually set eyes on the gory spectacle. Three weeks later, on September 21, the monarchy was declared abolished, and the new National Convention the official government of France. As non-royals, Louis and his family were required to use a surname; thenceforth, the former king would be known simply as "Louis Capet".

In December of 1792, Louis was separated from his family and friends and taken to trial for crimes against the First French Republic. A death sentence was pronounced against him on January 16th of the new year. For a few days, there was talk of a reprieve, or a pardon, but on January 20th, Louis was informed that he was to be guillotined at two in the afternoon on the following day. He asked for permission to see his family and bid them goodbye, and it was granted. By the time Louis was reunited with his wife, children, and sister, they had already heard the dire news from the town criers in the square below the Tower. Marie Antoinette led the family down into Louis's apartments, and begged him to let them stay the whole night with him. But Louis, who was overcome with emotion—he had asked his judges to protect his family, but he knew how unlikely it was that his son, or his wife, would survive him for long—said that he needed several hours alone in order to ready his mind and prepare his soul for death. Marie Antoinette and the children only agreed to leave him when he promised to come and see them in the morning for one final farewell. "Be sure that I shall see you again at eight o'clock tomorrow morning," he said.

"Why not seven o'clock?" said Marie Antoinette.

"Seven o'clock, then."

"Do you promise?"

"I promise."

But these were the last words he would ever speak to his family. He could not bring himself to visit them again the next morning. Marie Antoinette, Madame Elisabeth, and the children passed a sleepless night; then, the next afternoon, they listened to the deathlike hush that had fallen over the city. All at once, an enormous cry of joy went up: the King was dead, and the people were rejoicing. Marie Antoinette could do nothing but sink silently into a chair, while her children burst into sobs. Madame Elisabeth muttered to herself that the "monsters" would be "satisfied now".

She was, of course, entirely mistaken.

The trial of Marie Antoinette

The death of Louis inspired a depth of grief in Marie Antoinette that rendered her almost as indolent as her husband had once famously been. She could not seem to find relief in sharp bursts of agonized weeping or hysterics; she remained composed, numb, almost dulled to the horror that her life had become.

In the eyes of some, little Louis Charles was now the rightful King, Louis XVII of France. But to most, he was only the fatherless son of the woman now known as the Widow Capet. Powerful, humiliated, imprisoned, Marie Antoinette was still the most hated woman in France—a symbol, almost more so than Louis had been, of the *ancien régime,* and all that was hateful about the monarchy. There were some who wanted her tried immediately for crimes against the state. But even though history was full of kings who had lost their heads after losing the love of their people, and even though their sons and heirs were usually targets as well due to the fear that they would grow up to avenge their fathers, queens consort had always been spared the worst. The only queen executed in modern European history was Mary, Queen of Scots, and she had been a queen in her own right—and even so, it took another queen, Elizabeth I of England, to execute her. Chivalry did not always spare royal women indignity, but when men were in charge of their fate, it usually spared their lives.

But history had set out on a new course. The eighteenth century had produced enlightenment with one hand and revolution with the other; the old order was being swept away, and a modern sort of ruthlessness, based on political realities rather than ideals, was taking hold. As Robespierre and other architects of the Terror pointed out, the Widow Capet held no special status and was entitled to no special protections. She was no more than an ordinary citizen of the French Republic, and like all other citizens, she was liable to be tried for any crime she was accused of. Such friends as Marie Antoinette had left, including Axel Fersen, attempted to sell the idea of her being sent away from France. Her brother, Leopold, was dead, and her nephew, Francis, had succeeded him as Emperor; might he not claim her, as a "private person", so that she might end her days in peace, making no further trouble for France? The philosopher Thomas Paine suggested that she be sent to the United States. Both proposals were abandoned, however.

Then, in April of 1793, the Committee for Public Safety was formed. Composed of nine members, dominated by Robespierre, it was to assume the executive functions of government for the next two years. The Committee was stacked with men who wanted to see Marie Antoinette publicly tried and executed. In July of that year, the Committee decided to separate Louis Charles from his mother and put him in a different part of the Tower, so that he might be re-educated and forced to adopt the ideals of the Revolution. Education of any kind played little role in his life from that point forward, however. He was routinely abused by his guards, and from her own rooms, Marie Antoinette could hear him crying. Unbeknownst to her, the guards were forcing Louis Charles to say what they wanted to hear—namely, that his mother had forced him to participate in acts of incest. It was the sort of thing that a reader of pamphlets might easily believe, and the charge was expected to produce a dramatic effect at the former queen's trial.

At two o'clock in the morning, on August 1, 1793, Marie Antoinette was pulled from her rooms at the Tower and transferred to a squalid one-room cell at the nearby prison of the Conciergerie. Her daughter, Marie Therese, was left behind with her aunt, Madame Elisabeth. As "Prisoner no. 280", the former Queen of France—frail, her beauty gone, her hair entirely white at the age of 37—met with a kind reception from the wife of the chief jailer, who struggled to make her as comfortable as possible. Marie Antoinette retained a touching faith in her Austrian relations, and thought there was still a good chance that her nephew, Francis II, would ransom her or save her by some other means. And indeed, many of his ministers were pleading with him to do so. But Francis had never met his aunt, and was more or less indifferent to her plight.

By August of 1793, it was already too late to save her, though no one except the members of the Committee of Public Safety knew it yet. One of the members, Jacques Hébert, convinced the others that the ritual slaughter of the woman who symbolized France's last meaningful ties to the monarchy would bind the *sans-culottes,* the peasants who had taken up arms in the name of the new Republic, to the Committee in loyalty. They wanted to see the former Queen dead, and Hébert had told them they soon would. "I have promised the head of Antoinette," he proclaimed. (The abolishment of Roman Catholicism meant that the name "Marie", which honored the Virgin, was summarily dropped from her name.) "I will go and cut it off myself if there is any delay in giving it to me. I have promised it on your behalf to the *sans-culottes*, who are asking for it, *and without whom you will cease to be*." In other words, if the Widow Capet were not delivered up to the armed mob roaming the streets of Paris, that same mob might come for the Committee next.

As the widow Antoinette Capet, she was summoned to trial before the Revolutionary Tribunal on October

14, 1793. The outcome of the trial was pre-ordained; it was halfway over before she was even offered legal counsel, though Louis had been allowed to confer with lawyers throughout his trial. In every way, the trial of Marie Antoinette was harsher and more brutal than the trial of her husband had been. Chivalry, like Catholicism and kings, had been swept out the door by the new brooms of the Revolution.

In some ways, the trial of Marie Antoinette was her final moment of glory, though it certainly did not appear as such to anyone who was present in the courtroom. She had not been glimpsed by the general public since the disgraceful return from Varennes in 1791. In that time, she had taken on the appearance of an elderly woman, much older than her years—she would not live to see her 38th birthday, though it was only two weeks away. Her face was gaunt and sunken, her color ghastly, her hair white and brittle, her dress, plain black mourning garb which had been patched many times. Only by her immense composure and dignity might anyone have guessed that she was anything other than an unfortunate peasant woman.

The transcript of her trial demonstrates one thing quite clearly. However guilty she may have been as a younger woman of frivolity and inattention to her studies, she was an intelligent woman, and if cleverness could have saved her, she would probably have been acquitted:

"Q. It was remarked to her, that, not contented with dilapidating in a shocking manner the finances of France, the fruits of the sweat of the people, for the sake of her pleasures and intrigues, in concert with infamous ministers, she had sent to the Emperor thousands of millions, to serve against the nation which fostered her.

A. Never; that she knows that this mean has frequently been made subservient against her; that she loved her husband too much to dilapidate the money of his country; that her brother did not want money from France; and that, from the same principles which attached her to this country, she would not have given him any.

Q. Observed, that, since the revolution, she has not ceased an instant to carry on maneuvers with the foreign powers, even at a period when we only had the image of that liberty which the French nation absolutely wishes for.

A. That, since the revolution, she had forborne all foreign correspondence; that she never meddled in domestic concerns.

Q. Whether she did not employ some secret agent to correspond with the foreign powers, chiefly with her brothers...?

A. Never in her life.

Q. Observed, that it was she who taught Louis Capet that art of profound dissimulation by which he had

177

too long deceived the kind French nation, who did not suppose that perfidy and villainy could be carried to such a degree.

A. Yes, the people have been deceived—cruelly deceived! but it was neither by her nor her husband.

Q. By whom, then, has the people been deceived?

A. By those who felt it in their interest; that it had never been theirs to deceive them.

Q. Observed, that she did not answer directly the question.

A. That she would answer it directly if she knew the names of the persons.

Q. Observed, that she was the principal instigatrix to the treason of Louis Capet; that it was by her advice, and perhaps by her importunities and teasing, that he resolved to fly France, to put himself at the head of the furious men who wished to tear his country.

A. That her husband did not wish to quit France; that she followed him on his journey; that she would have followed him every-where; but that if she had known that he wanted to quit his country, she would have employed all possible means to dissuade him; but that he had no such intention.

Q. Why did you travel at that period by the borrowed name of a Russian baroness?

A. Because we could not get out of Paris without changing name.

Q. Observed, that she never concealed for a moment her desire of destroying liberty; that she wanted to reign at any rate, and re-ascend the throne upon the corpses of patriots.

A. That they did not want to re-ascend the throne: That they were upon it; that they never had any other desire but the happiness of France. Be it happy; be it but happy! they would always be contented.

Q. What interest does she take in the success of the armies of the republic?

A. The happiness of France is what she desires above all things.

Q. Do you think that kings are necessary to the happiness of the people?

A. An individual could not positively decide such a matter.

Q. You regret, without a doubt, that your son has lost a throne which he might have ascended, if the people, at length enlightened upon their true rights, had not themselves crushed that throne?

A. She shall never regret anything for her son, so long as her country is happy."

Many of her answers were, clearly, lies. She had indeed presided over "secret and nocturnal petty councils". She had done everything in her power to convince Louis to escape to Austria; she had written letters to many foreign officials; she had wanted nothing more than to see the Revolution destroyed, the monarchy restored, and her son seated on his father's throne in the fullness of time. But she knew that the tribunal had no concrete evidence of any of these treasons.

But much of her testimony was the simple truth. She was accused of political intrigues, but she was also accused of crimes that only the most perverse imagination could devise. For years, the pamphlet industry had been convincing the people of France that she was a vain, sexually insatiable woman who had betrayed her husband countless times with innumerable lovers, both men and women; that she had willfully drained the coffers of the nation to fund her appetite for luxury; that she was a foreign agent who wanted nothing more than to destroy France and promote the glory of Austria. Most of the accusations leveled against her at her trial were fantasies which had originally appeared in those pamphlets. She was so accustomed to these calumnies that she could scarcely summon any outrage over them. But then, Jacques Hébert produced the incest charge which had been wrested from Louis Charles, "the young Capet", by torture and abuse. He told the courtroom that she and Madame Elisabeth had engaged in *pollutions indécents* with the eight-year old boy, and that the older women had forced him to engage in incestuous acts with his sister.

To these accusations, Marie Antoinette made no reply at first. When an answer was insisted upon, the room went silent; no one wanted to miss a word. When she spoke, she was no longer resigned and composed.

Her voice trembled with emotion. "If I have not replied," she said, "it is because Nature itself refuses to respond to such a charge against a mother." To the commoners in the galleries, she cried out: "I appeal to all mothers who may be present." There came a loud response from the women in the room, and the judges of the Tribunal swiftly perceived that the bomb they had just detonated had backfired. No further mention was made of the incest charge.

Since no one but the Committee members knew that the trial, which lasted for two days and a night, was only for show, the general verdict was that the former queen had "answered like an angel", and that she would be allowed to leave the country unharmed. Marie Antoinette herself was convinced that, since nothing had been proven against her, she would be released, or ransomed. She retained that conviction until the official verdict was reached—at four in the morning, on October 16th. Summoned back to the courtroom, she was handed the paper on which the verdict was written, and told that the death sentence had been asked for, and would be granted. She would be executed in eight hours' time, at noon. Had she any last words to say? Marie Antoinette shook her head. Though she was undoubtedly in a state of profound shock, it did not show. To onlookers, who saw her lift her head high as she exited the courtroom, the former Queen of France appeared to be in a trancelike state.

A half hour later, in her rooms, she was permitted paper and pen so that she might write a letter of farewell to her sister-in-law, Madame Elisabeth. The letter was never delivered; Elisabeth did not learn that Marie Antoinette had been executed until after she herself was condemned to the same fate in May of 1794.

"16th October, 4.30 A.M.

It is to you, my sister, that I write for the last time. I have just been condemned, not to a shameful death, for such is only for criminals, but to go and rejoin your brother. Innocent like him, I hope to show the

184

same firmness in my last moments. I am calm, as one is when one's conscience reproaches one with nothing. I feel profound sorrow in leaving my poor children: you know that I only lived for them and for you, my good and tender sister. You who out of love have sacrificed everything to be with us, in what a position do I leave you! I have learned from the proceedings at my trial that my daughter was separated from you. Alas! poor child; I do not venture to write to her; she would not receive my letter. I do not even know whether this will reach you. Do you receive my blessing for both of them. I hope that one day when they are older they may be able to rejoin you, and to enjoy to the full your tender care. Let them both think of the lesson which I have never ceased to impress upon them, that the principles and the exact performance of their duties are the chief foundation of life; and then mutual affection and confidence in one another will constitute its happiness. Let my daughter feel that at her age she ought always to aid her brother by the advice which her greater

experience and her affection may inspire her to give him. And let my son in his turn render to his sister all the care and all the services which affection can inspire. Let them, in short, both feel that, in whatever positions they may be placed, they will never be truly happy but through their union. Let them follow our example. In our own misfortunes how much comfort has our affection for one another afforded us! And, in times of happiness, we have enjoyed that doubly from being able to share it with a friend; and where can one find friends more tender and more united than in one's own family? Let my son never forget the last words of his father, which I repeat emphatically; let him never seek to avenge our deaths.

I have to speak to you of one thing which is very painful to my heart, I know how much pain the child must have caused you. Forgive him, my dear sister; think of his age, and how easy it is to make a child say whatever one wishes, especially when he does not understand it. It will come to pass one day, I hope, that he will better feel the value of your kindness and of your tender affection for both of them. It remains to confide to you my last thoughts. I should have wished to write them at the beginning of my trial; but, besides that they did not leave me any means of writing, events have passed so rapidly that I really have not had time.

I die in the Catholic Apostolic and Roman religion, that of my fathers, that in which I was brought up, and which I have always professed. Having no spiritual consolation to look for, not even knowing whether there are still in this place any priests of that religion (and indeed the place where I am would expose them to too much danger if they were to enter it but once), I sincerely implore pardon of God for all the faults which I may have committed during my life. I trust that, in His goodness, He will mercifully accept my last prayers, as well as those which I have for a long time addressed to Him, to receive my soul into His mercy. I beg pardon of all whom I know, and especially of you, my sister, for all the vexations which, without intending it, I may have caused you. I pardon all my enemies the evils that they have done me. I bid farewell to my aunts and to all my brothers and sisters. I had friends. The idea of being forever separated from them and from all their troubles is one of the greatest sorrows that I suffer in dying. Let them at least know that to my latest moment I thought of them.

Farewell, my good and tender sister. May this letter reach you. Think always of me; I embrace you with all my heart, as I do my poor dear children. My God, how heart-rending it is to leave them forever! Farewell! farewell! I must now occupy myself with my spiritual duties, as I am not free in my actions. Perhaps they will bring me a priest; but I here protest that I will not say a word to him, but that I will treat him as a total stranger."

The death of Marie Antoinette

The procession which brought the last Queen of France to her death was deliberately slow. Marie Antoinette should "drink long of death", it had been decided. Sitting on a box in the back of a cart, she was driven at such a leisurely pace that everyone who had lined up to see her, including the 30,000 soldiers standing guard, had ample time to study the woman who, for so long, had existed only in their imaginations. There were two Marie Antoinettes, people believed; sometimes she was the glittering queen who reigned over a court of unimaginable luxury, callous and indifferent to the suffering of her people, and sometimes she was the bloodthirsty monster who had come to France for the express purpose of feeding its people to the Austrian war machine. But the woman who was being brought to the guillotine that day did not look like anything very extraordinary. She was not allowed to dress in her mourning garb, so she wore the only other dress she had, a simple white gown. In previous centuries, white had been the mourning color of the Queens of France, but no one seemed to have remembered that. She was so unremarkable looking now that, had she been permitted to slip away from her captors, she could easily have disappeared into the crowd. The daughter of the great Austrian empress was now just another haggard woman, aged beyond her years, who had learned a good deal about cruelty and suffering in a short amount of time. Just shy of her 38th birthday, she would be younger when she died than her mother the Empress had been when she gave birth to her.

Those who had condemned her to death hoped that she would give the crowd a good show—that she would scream or weep or beg for mercy. Already, she had been humiliated to the greatest extent possible. Her thin white hair had been cut very short, and her hands were bound high and tight behind her back. Instead of being conveyed to the place of execution in a carriage, she was taken in a cart, and told to sit with her back to the horses. Yet, this ordeal, which lasted for an hour—she was taken from her cell at eleven o'clock—did not seem to touch her. She had already gone somewhere else in her mind. Once, as a child, she had laughed at the priests who tried to make her devout, but in recent years she had come to take deep consolation from her Catholic faith; perhaps she was praying, or imagining the world to come.

Some thought that her composure betokened arrogance. Hébert, whose rancor against Marie Antoinette was so pronounced that it seems almost to have been personal, would say later that, "the whore was audacious and insolent to the very end." But others gave her due credit for her immense dignity; one revolutionary newspaper went so far as to admit that she showed "courage enough". One observer to her death was the envoy of Parma, where Marie Antoinette's sister was Duchess: "Marie Antoinette never failed for a single instant either her great soul or the illustrious blood of the House of Austria."

By the time the cart bearing Marie Antoinette reached the place of execution, she seemed to have gained a little energy. Though her hands were bound behind her back, she got down from the cart and mounted the steps of the scaffold without assistance. Briefly, she paused to apologize to the executioner for having stepped on his foot: "Pardon me, monsieur. I did not do it on purpose." Her only companion on the scaffold was a republican priest, whose spiritual services she had refused. "This is the moment, Madame, to arm yourself with courage," he told her.

"Courage!" she cried, with some surprise. "The moment when my ills are going to end is not the moment courage is going to fail me."

At fifteen minutes after twelve, the blade of the guillotine fell, bestowing its gift of painless death. The head of Marie Antoinette was held high above the crowd, to exclamations and cheers. But she did not hear them.

Other great books by Michael W. Simmons on Kindle, paperback and audio:

Elizabeth I: Legendary Queen Of England

Alexander Hamilton: First Architect Of The American Government

William Shakespeare: An Intimate Look Into The Life Of The Most Brilliant Writer In The History Of The English Language

Thomas Edison: American Inventor

Catherine the Great: Last Empress of Russia

Romanov: The Last Tsarist Dynasty

Peter the Great: Autocrat and Reformer

The Rothschilds: The Dynasty and the Legacy

Queen Victoria: Icon of an Era

Six Wives: The Women Who Married, Lived, and
Died for Henry VIII

John D. Rockefeller: The Wealthiest Man in
American History

Princess to Queen: The Early Years of Queen
Elizabeth II

Queen of People's Hearts: The Life and Mission of
Diana, Princess of Wales

Jackie Kennedy Onassis: The Widow of Camelot

Ulysses S. Grant: The War Years

Further Reading

Marie Antoinette: The Journey, by Antonia Fraser

The Guardian of Marie Antoinette: letters from the Comte de Mercy-Argenteau, Austrian ambassador to the court of Versailles, to Marie Therese, empress of Austria, 1770-1780

> https://archive.org/stream/guardianofmariea01smyt/guardianofmariea01smyt_djvu.txt

Memoirs of the private life of Marie Antoinette, queen of France and Navarre, by Mme. Jeanne-Louise-Henriette Campan

> https://play.google.com/store/books/details?id=JjMOAAAAQAAJ&rdid=book-JjMOAAAAQAAJ&rdot=1

The Life of Jane de St. Remy de Valois, Heretofore Countess de La Motte

> https://play.google.com/books/reader?id=PVQvAAAAMAAJ&printsec=frontcover&output=reader&hl=en&pg=GBS.PA1

Letter from Marie Antoinette to Maria Teresa of Austria

https://sourcebooks.fordham.edu/mod/1773 marieantonette.asp

"The Truth About Louis XVI's Marital Difficulties"

http://www.historyofcircumcision.net/index. php?option=content&task=view&id=78

The Constitution of 1791

http://www.historywiz.com/primarysources/ const1791text.html

Final letter of Marie Antoinette

http://teaattrianon.blogspot.com/2007/05/la st-letter-of-marie-antoinette.html

Authentic Trial at Large of Marie Antoinette, Late Queen of France, before the Revolutionary Tribunal, at Paris

https://docs.google.com/viewer?url=http://cultureandstuff.com/Authentic_Trial_at_Large_of_Marie_Antoinette_via_Cultureandstuff.pdf&pli=1&chrome=true

Made in the USA
Columbia, SC
02 December 2018